T0150445

THE
P.G. Wodehouse
MISCELLANY

THE
P.G. Wodehouse
MISCELLANY

N. T. P. MURPHY

The
History
Press

First published 2015

The History Press
The Mill, Brimscombe Port
Stroud, Gloucestershire, GL5 2QG
www.thehistorypress.co.uk

British Library Cataloguing in Publication Data.
A catalogue record for this book is available from the British Library.

ISBN 978 0 7509 5964 3

Typesetting and origination by The History Press
Printed in Europe

· CONTENTS ·

• ACKNOWLEDGEMENTS •

My thanks go first of all to the Wodehouse Estate for allowing me to quote from Wodehouse's books and letters, and to Sir Edward Cazalet for permission to use pictures from his collection. I am also grateful to Mrs Calista Lucy, Keeper of the Archive at Dulwich College, for her assistance in obtaining other photos.

I am deeply indebted to Stephen Fry, whose great admiration for Wodehouse has inspired many enthusiasts and is so well expressed in his foreword.

I wish to express my gratitude to Neil Midkiff, who was kind enough to go through the manuscript and made many invaluable suggestions and corrections. Thanks are also due to Jean Tillson and to my son for pointing out errors that might otherwise have slipped through.

Finally, I owe a debt of gratitude to my wife, Elin, without whose guidance and editorial expertise this book would never have reached fruition.

NORMAN MURPHY'S CREDENTIALS AS the finest writer on Wodehouse since the sad death of Richard Usborne need no affirmation from me. This, dash it, is the man who found out exactly where Blandings Castle is. Such an act of benevolent scholarship assures his immortality. A new book from him is always a treat.

There are many collections of the various worlds and characters that Wodehouse dreamt up: Psmith, Blandings, Ukridge, the Hollywood tales, Mr Mulliner and his roster of feckless nephews, the adventures of the members of the Drones Club — Oofy Prosser, Boko, Bingo and Pongo (whose disgraceful and eternally sprightly Uncle Fred is a sub-category to himself) — and of course the ever-resourceful Jeeves respectfully helping his 'mentally negligible' young master Bertie out of the soup time and time again. It is common to clump the collections together, as Wodehouse himself often did. *Young Men in Spats* and *Eggs, Beans and Crumpets*, for example, unveiled the adventures of Drones members, Freddie Widgeon being an especial star member of that cast of charming but distinctly uncerebral young asses. *The Clicking of Cuthbert* and *The Heart of a Goof* contain the best golfing stories ever written. Stanley Featherstonehaugh Ukridge (pronounced Stanley Fanshaw Ewkridge) is delineated in *Love Among the Chickens* and *Ukridge* as well as appearing in *Lord Emsworth and Others,* where naturally that dreamy peer and his fretful sister Connie also appear. The fact of the matter is that Wodehouse was so prodigious and had such a cast to play with that the criss-crossings and popping-up of so many characters in varying Wodehousian milieux make Norman Murphy's miscellany the perfect introduction to the whole Wodehousiness of Wodehouse.

I am always delighted more than I can say that the series *Jeeves and Wooster* that I appeared in over a quarter of a century ago with my friend Hugh Laurie still causes people to come up to me and say that it was this that turned them to reading the works of the Master. There can have been no greater a mission or purpose. He lives entirely on the page. While a stage or screen adaptation may or may not appeal to some, there can be no doubt at all such versions can never match the utter delirious joy of the prose.

What a service Norman Murphy has done those who have perhaps only dipped their toe in Jeeves and Wooster, or taken a teaspoonful or so of Blandings. There is so much more to enjoy. This little book, I guarantee, will cause you to turn to the bookshop or library and grab heaping handfuls of stories that will enrich and entrance you for ever.

· INTRODUCTION ·

P.G. WODEHOUSE DIED IN 1975 but is still widely read around the world. While there are those who say his writing is pure escapist fiction, as indeed it is, others point out that he shared the literary stage of the 1920s and '30s with such writers as W.W. Jacobs, Rudyard Kipling, Arnold Bennett, John Buchan, Sapper (H.C. McNeile), Dornford Yates and Edgar Wallace. Their names are remembered today – but how many people actually read their books? Millions still read Wodehouse – why?

Perhaps the first clue can be found in the list of his admirers. These included such contemporary luminaries as Prime Minister Herbert Asquith; classical scholar and poet A.E. Housman; philosopher Bertrand Russell; and fellow authors Hilaire Belloc, George Orwell and W.H. Auden. Modern admirers include Hugh Laurie and Stephen Fry (who played Bertie Wooster and Jeeves on television), Andrew Lloyd Webber and Alan Ayckbourn (who created the musical *By Jeeves*), actor Simon Callow and author Lynne Truss, among many others.

Wodehouse enthusiasts realise that while other authors dealt with serious subjects in plain English, Wodehouse did the opposite. He wrote intricately plotted light comedies with splendid humorous metaphors and a constant flow of literary references and quotations – and superb deliberate misquotations – ranging from the Bible and Homer, through Shakespeare, Dickens and Gilbert & Sullivan, to contemporary popular songs, advertisements and clichés of the day. He made his readers laugh, not just by the stories he wrote but by the way he wrote them. As Allan Massie wrote in *The Scotsman* (14 January 1984):

> Wodehouse is, with the possible exception of Joyce, the most literary of our great novelists. He is not only highly allusive, but his work offers a continuous succession of various themes from the Bible, Shakespeare and other poets. This is perhaps the one obstacle to his survival for the way education is going, it must be doubtful if anyone will be able to

understand him in a couple of generations without the myriad footnotes now provided for works like the Dunciad.

Finally, he is not only the most literary, but – again Joyce is the only rival – the most completely devoted to literature.

Wodehouse earned his first half-guinea for an article, 'Some Aspects of Game-Captaincy' (*Public School Magazine*, February 1900), while he was still at school. Over the next seventy-five years, he never stopped writing. His ninety-eight books – mainly novels and short stories – feature a vast range of characters, of whom probably the best known are the amiable and well-meaning, if ineffectual, Bertie Wooster and his omniscient manservant Jeeves. In a series of short stories and novels, Jeeves rescues Bertie from a succession of predicaments, usually caused by an interfering aunt or an accidentally acquired fiancée. Jeeves' ultra-correct and formal speech contrasts superbly with Bertie's contemporary slang mixed with half-remembered Latin tags and Shakespearean quotations from his school days.

In the Blandings Castle stories, we read of the trials and tribulations of the absent-minded Lord Emsworth, who only wants to lead a quiet life and look after his prize pig, Empress of Blandings. This ambition is continually thwarted by secretaries, head gardeners, and his many sisters involving him in the romantic affairs of his nephews and nieces.

Mr Mulliner presides over the bar parlour of the Anglers' Rest, and there is no topic of conversation that does not inspire him to narrate tall tales about his many relations. These range from timid curates in rural Worcestershire to assistant film producers in Hollywood.

The Oldest Member's golf stories emphasise the spell the game casts on its devotees and the effect it can have on their love lives.

The Drones Club tales recount the adventures and misadventures, financial and romantic, of various friends of Bertie Wooster.

The Ukridge short stories deal with the invariably unsuccessful financial schemes of the unscrupulous but eternally optimistic Stanley Ukridge. Ukridge's scruffy appearance is in sharp contrast to Rupert Psmith, whose elegance is equalled only by his mastery of difficult situations.

In addition to these, Wodehouse wrote a number of school stories and many light romances. He also worked in the theatre for more than forty years, both as a playwright working with Guy Bolton and as a highly successful librettist/lyric writer for forty musical comedies. Several of his stories were made into films, and he spent two years as a scriptwriter in Hollywood.

A long, blameless and busy life was marred only by an unhappy incident that resulted in Wodehouse moving permanently to America in 1947. His last years were spent, as always, in writing, and his 80th and 90th birthdays brought tributes from around the world. The award of a well-deserved knighthood in 1975 delighted his admirers, but it was soon followed by the news of his death on St Valentine's Day 1975 with – as was only to be expected – a manuscript beside him. It was published posthumously as *Sunset at Blandings*.

Since his death, Wodehouse's popularity has grown thanks to the internet and the establishment of numerous Wodehouse Societies around the world. Wodehouse quotations and references occur daily in books, magazines, and newspapers – proof of the enduring popularity of a comic genius.

1

BIRTH AND BACKGROUND

THE WODEHOUSE FAMILY IS an old one; Sir John Wodehouse won his knighthood at the Battle of Agincourt in 1415. Established at Kimberley in Norfolk since the fifteenth century, the heads of the family served as Members of Parliament and were raised to a baronetcy in 1611. In 1797 they were promoted to the rank of baron, and in 1866 the head of the family was created the Earl of Kimberley. Wodehouse's grandfather, a grandson of the 3rd Baron, fought at Waterloo.

Pelham Grenville Wodehouse (known to his family and friends as 'Plum' throughout his life) was born on 15 October 1881 at 59 Epsom Road, Guildford, Surrey (there is now a plaque on the house). His mother, Eleanor Deane Wodehouse, home from Hong Kong, was staying with a sister a few miles away and was paying a social call on a friend when Wodehouse made his appearance. Soon afterwards, his mother took him out to Hong Kong, where her husband, Henry Ernest Wodehouse, was a magistrate. There the baby Pelham joined his two elder brothers, Philip Peveril (born 1877) and Ernest Armine (born 1879). A younger brother, Richard Lancelot, was born in 1892.

In 1883 the boys were brought back to England and put in the charge of a Miss Roper, who lived in Bath near Wodehouse's grandparents. In 1885–86 they became boarders at a small establishment run

Pelham Grenville Wodehouse (right) with his brothers Ernest Armine (left) and Philip Peveril (centre). (Courtesy of Sir Edward Cazalet and the Wodehouse Estate)

by two sisters, the Misses Prince, at The Chalet, St Peter's Road, South Croydon, which became today's Elmhurst School. After a short period at Elizabeth College, Guernsey, Plum was sent to a small school in Dover. It was named Malvern House – the name Wodehouse used later for the prep school attended by Bertie Wooster.

Because his parents were in Hong Kong, Wodehouse saw very little of them until he reached the age of 15. In those days, when travel to the Far East took several weeks, home leave was granted only every four years or so. And since there was no air conditioning and European children were very vulnerable to tropical diseases, they were sent home to be looked after by relatives. Today this seems heartless, but then it was common for children whose parents served in distant parts of the Empire. The result was that Wodehouse was looked after by a succession of aunts and uncles whom he came to know better than he did his own parents.

Since Wodehouse's father and mother both came from large families, he possessed no fewer than twenty aunts and fifteen uncles. These included four clergymen and many service officers and colonial administrators. Few were wealthy, but they were all what was then known as 'gentry' and were very conscious of the fact.

> *Where's your pride? Have you forgotten your
> illustrious ancestors? There was a Wooster at the time
> of the Crusades who would have won the Battle of
> Joppa single-handed, if he hadn't fallen off his horse.*
> *(Aunts Aren't Gentlemen)*

During much of his childhood, Wodehouse lived
at Cheney Court in Wiltshire, the home of his
grandmother and four spinster aunts. He recalled
accompanying his aunts when they paid formal calls
at the Big Houses in the area and the hostesses tactfully suggesting that young Pelham might prefer
to have his tea in the Servants' Hall. It gave him an
early insight into 'life below stairs' that he would
put to good use later.

When he came to live in London as a bank clerk
and, later, a young journalist, there were uncles and
aunts in Kensington and Knightsbridge who made
sure he fulfilled what they considered his social
obligations, whether he liked it or not. This meant
donning a top hat, frock coat, gloves and spats, and
accompanying his aunts when they paid formal calls
or attended 'At Homes', or attiring himself in evening dress (white tie and tails) to attend dinners

where the guests included members of the peerage and, on one occasion, an Italian prince. It was very different from his usual routine as a young freelance writer, but it was a social duty he could not avoid.

The influence of these uncles and aunts cannot be overestimated in Wodehouse's stories. He realised early on that an overbearing father or mother cannot be a figure of fun; an overbearing aunt or uncle can, and this became a permanent factor, especially in the stories featuring Bertie Wooster. In a letter (14 January 1955), he wrote: 'Aunt Agatha is definitely my Aunt Mary [Mary Deane] who was the scourge of my childhood.'

> *On the cue 'five aunts' I had given at the knees a trifle, for the thought of being confronted with such a solid gaggle of aunts, even if those of another, was an unnerving one. Reminding myself that in this life it is not aunts that matter, but the courage that one brings to them, I pulled myself together. (The Mating Season)*

Towards the end of his long life, Wodehouse freely admitted he was writing of a world that ended in 1914, a world of country houses, eccentric aristocrats and young men with menservants and nothing to do but enjoy themselves. But it was the world he had grown up in; what he did was to see the funny side of it and exaggerate features his readers would recognise.

While we think of Bertie Wooster and his friends as typical young men of the 1920s and '30s, that is because Wodehouse updated them so well. Their clothing, their sports cars and their speech change through the years, following faithfully the fashions of the day, and after 1945, in *Ring for Jeeves* and *Cocktail Time*, we read of the problems of those condemned to live in large country houses without the money to run them. But the same happy spirit runs through them all.

2

DULWICH AND THE BANK

> *From my earliest years I had always wanted to be a*
> *writer. I started turning out the stuff at the age of*
> *five. (What I was doing before that, I don't remember.*
> *Just loafing, I suppose.) (Over Seventy)*

ON 2 MAY 1894, Wodehouse entered Dulwich College, South London, which his brother Armine had entered two years earlier. Wodehouse loved the school from the moment he saw it and followed its fortunes for the rest of his life. Some have said he had a fixation on his old school and never grew out of it. Perhaps so, but it should be remembered Dulwich was his first real home. Until he was 15, he only saw his parents at three- or four-year intervals and never developed the normal child-parent bonds. Dulwich was the first stable environment he knew. It was a place with a routine of order and discipline – factors every boy needs. He was successful there; he became a prefect, played for the cricket and rugby teams, boxed, and was an editor of the school magazine *The Alleynian*.

Years later, Wodehouse noted how lucky he had been to attend in what was a golden period for the school. The headmaster, A.H. Gilkes, inspired not only the staff but the boys as well, and Dulwich became known for the number of scholarships it won to Oxford and Cambridge. Wodehouse was not alone in his affection for Dulwich; a remarkable number of boys went to university and promptly returned to their old school as teachers. When Wodehouse was living in London, he attended every important Dulwich rugby and cricket match and later arranged his trips from France to coincide with such matches. He also used the area immediately around the school as Valley Fields, a setting for many of his later stories.

> *From the fact that he spoke as if he had a hot potato in his mouth without getting the raspberry from the lads in the ringside seats, I deduced he must be the headmaster. (Right Ho, Jeeves)*

A young Wodehouse on the cricket pitch at Dulwich College. (With kind permission of the Governors of Dulwich College)

> '*You don't know anything about anything,*' Mr. Pynsent
> pointed out gently. '*It is the effect of your English
> public-school education.*' (*Sam the Sudden*)

One of the school libraries is now named after
him, and his desk and typewriter stand in one corner.

In his last year at Dulwich (1899–1900),
Wodehouse was working hard for a scholarship
to Oxford. In early 1900, however, his father
informed him he would be unable to pay the university fees and had secured a place for him as a
clerk at the Hong Kong and Shanghai Bank, which
trained its managerial staff in London. After a few
years in the Lombard Street office, they went out
to the Far East as assistant managers. Most of the
young clerks were, like Wodehouse, from public
schools, and although he claimed he never really
got to terms with the technical side of banking, he
played rugby and cricket for the bank and got on
well with his fellows.

But he was determined to make his living as a
writer and spent his evenings writing articles on
schools like Malvern and Tonbridge for *The Public*

School Magazine and such topics as football at Dulwich. They did not bring in much money, perhaps half a guinea each, but the average wage then was about £1.40 a week.

He also began submitting humorous pieces and verses to newspapers and magazines. He was fortunate in his market. There was no radio, film or television then, and there were over 700 weekly and monthly 'story' magazines in the UK, while London had nineteen morning and ten evening papers.

Perceval Graves, elder brother of the poet Robert Graves, shared lodgings in Walpole Street, Chelsea, with Wodehouse and remembered him leaving the table immediately after the evening meal and writing, writing, writing in the bathroom until midnight. In August 1901 he went to see W. Beach-Thomas, who had been a Dulwich master and who was then working on the 'By The Way' column of *The Globe* evening newspaper. Wodehouse secured an occasional day's work on the column and continued to submit jokes and short articles to a wide variety of magazines. In September 1902 he was offered five weeks' work on *The Globe*, upon which he made the decision to leave the bank and become a freelance writer.

He was not yet 21 years old, but the first of what were to be many contributions to *Punch* appeared on 17 September 1902, followed by the publication of his first book, *The Pothunters*, the next day. Over the next eleven months his work appeared in many magazines and he secured more work on *The Globe's* 'By The Way' column, culminating in the offer of regular employment in August 1903. He was on his way.

3

THE GLOBE, THE SCHOOL STORIES AND PSMITH

THE 'BY THE WAY' column appeared on the front page of *The Globe*, a London evening newspaper, and consisted of humorous comments on topics of the day. It was written by at least two, sometimes three, people and it is extremely difficult now to identify Wodehouse's contributions.

The column normally began with some satirical comment on speeches made by Liberal politicians (*The Globe* was a Conservative paper). This was followed by reports of incidents in the news with some amusing comment on them. For example, when George Edwardes of the Gaiety Theatre complained of a group booing at a first night, the column declared that it 'was taboo to boo'. Since everybody knew General Bosquet's description of the charge of the Light Brigade at Balaklava, '*C'est magnifique, mais ce n'est pas la guerre*', the news that the French government was reducing the strength of beer was promptly greeted with: '*C'est magnifique, mais ce n'est pas lager.*' When the Emir of Kano in Nigeria declared war on Britain, the column assumed that most of its readers had done Latin at school and would therefore recognise the opening lines of Virgil's *Aeneid*: '*Arma virumque cano*' (Of arms and the man, I sing). So, after reporting the declaration of war, the comment was simply 'Emir Virumque Kano'.

It seems easy, but the column required discipline and concentration. The copy had to be with the printer by noon. This meant arriving punctually, reading the morning papers, picking out selected items and working out a humorous comment on them, often in verse. The requirement to write humorous light verses against time on any given topic undoubtedly developed Wodehouse's remarkable skill in writing lyrics for musical comedy, which would later be employed with great success.

In *Not George Washington* (1907), a semi-autobiographical novel based on his time at *The Globe*, Wodehouse wrote how valuable the experience had been:

I had learned the art of writing against time. I had learned to ignore noise, which, for a writer in London, is the most valuable quality of all. All this gave me a power of concentration, without which writing is difficult in this city of noises.

After midday, Wodehouse's time was his own, and since *The Globe* did not object to his submitting work elsewhere, he took full advantage, turning out short stories for magazines and writing topical lyrics for songs interpolated into musical comedies. One of these, *The Beauty of Bath* (1906), had two songs written by a young American named Jerome Kern, with whom Wodehouse would work again later. His income grew steadily from his school stories, which first appeared in the boys' magazine *The Captain*. *The Pothunters*, which came out in 1902, was followed by *A Prefect's Uncle* (1903), *Tales of St Austin's* (1903), *The Gold Bat* (1904), *The Head of Kay's* (1905), *The White Feather* (1907) and *Mike* (1909).

'Are you the Bully, the Pride of the School, or the Boy who is Led Astray and Takes to Drink in Chapter Sixteen?' (Mike)

The books were very popular, since schoolboys found them different from the 'moral and improving' school stories that were still common. Wodehouse wrote them from a boy's point of view, and such moral principles as he expressed were those boys approved of. You didn't tell tales to get another boy into trouble; you might cheat in your daily schoolwork but never in an examination. If you slacked in your schoolwork, nobody minded, but slacking at games was a different matter. If you were playing for your school, you tried your hardest; nothing else was accepted.

Wodehouse used the routine of Dulwich for his stories, and some of his characters are directly traceable to Dulwich colleagues. In *The Head of Kay's*, the schoolboy Fenn was based on N.A. Knox, who played in the First XI with Wodehouse and later went on to play for England. Embittered by his housemaster's treatment, Fenn reduces a school concert to chaos by playing a noisy jazz piece on the piano, clapped and cheered loudly by the whole school over the calls for order from the headmaster.

In *Mike*, a boy leads the school on a day's march around the local countryside in protest against the headmaster. Every contemporary reader recognised the reference to the famous march-out by Haileybury School. One of the major events of the

Boer War was the Relief of Ladysmith, and when British forces raised the siege there was widespread rejoicing and many schools granted a half-holiday. The headmaster of Haileybury refused, so the school took one anyway. It was led by a boy named C.R. Attlee, who was later to succeed Winston Churchill as prime minister.

In 1896 Wodehouse's parents came back from Hong Kong and took a house in Dulwich, before moving to the hamlet of Stableford, near Bridgnorth in Shropshire. Wodehouse loved it, transposing Dulwich to Shropshire and setting his fictional school 'Wrykyn' there. Wodehouse used many local names in his stories: for example, Roughton becomes 'Rutton', while Ackleton becomes 'Eckleton'. 'Badger Dingle', where the boys look for birds' nests, is Badgwick Dingle, about half a mile from Wodehouse's Stableford home.

In *The Gold Bat*, he 'moved' Wrykyn again, using Shrewsbury School as a model. In *Mike*, he moved it again and based it unmistakeably on Malvern College. Mike Jackson and his cricketing brothers are equally unmistakeably based on the seven Foster brothers of Malvern. All seven played for their county; one, R.E. Foster, is the only man to have captained England at both cricket and football.

In *Mike*, Wodehouse introduced his first comedy character, the tall, languid schoolboy Rupert Psmith, based on what a cousin had told him about a fellow schoolboy at Winchester, Rupert D'Oyly Carte. Psmith's elegance, his monocle and his air of kindly condescension, whether he is addressing a schoolfellow or a headmaster, made him instantly popular with boys. *Psmith in the City* came out a year later (1910); this was followed by Psmith's adventures in New York (*Psmith, Journalist*). Later, Wodehouse's stepdaughter, Leonora, persuaded him to write *Leave It to Psmith*, in which Psmith became one of the many impostors to visit Blandings Castle.

Rupert Psmith is important in Wodehouse's writing. He was his first major humorous character and acted as a bridge between the school stories and the world of Bertie Wooster and the Drones Club. Until well into the 1920s, Wodehouse was best known as 'the creator of Psmith'.

4

EMSWORTH AND STANLEY FEATHERSTONEHAUGH UKRIDGE

IN 1903 A YOUNG man called on Wodehouse with a letter of introduction. Herbert Wotton Westbrook had come down from Cambridge and become an assistant master at a prep school run by Baldwin King-Hall at Emsworth, a small seaside town on the Sussex–Hampshire border. They became friends, and Westbrook invited Wodehouse to stay at the school. Wodehouse liked Emsworth and rented a house backing onto the school grounds.

Emsworth played a significant part in Wodehouse's writing. He used it as a setting for some short stories, and *The Little Nugget* (1913), which revolves around attempts to kidnap the unpleasant son of an American millionaire, is set in a prep school for boys. Because American gang-sters in a quiet English village would be unrealistic, Wodehouse placed the school in a large house a couple of miles away, which he called 'Sanstead House'. His description of the house and grounds fits exactly with a stately home just a few miles from Emsworth – Stansted Park. The house appears again as Belpher Castle in *A Damsel in Distress* (1919).

But Emsworth's greatest legacy in Wodehouse's writing was his use of local names for the family living in the earthly paradise we know as Blandings Castle. In the first Blandings novel, *Something Fresh* (1915), Lord Emsworth was named after Emsworth itself while the family name, Threepwood, is the name of Wodehouse's house in Record Road, Emsworth. The blue plaque over the front door today was unveiled in 1995 by Ian Carmichael, who had played Bertie Wooster on TV in the 1960s alongside Dennis Price as Jeeves.

Lord Emsworth's brother-in-law, Colonel Mant, takes his name from the four Mant brothers, who were important members of the Emsworth com-munity. At its southern end, Record Road faces Beach Road, which gave its name to the Blandings butler. Lord Emsworth's heir, Lord Bosham, takes his name from Bosham, a village to the east of

The plaque on Threepwood, the house where Wodehouse lived in Emsworth.

Emsworth; his sister, Lady Ann Warblington, is named after a hamlet a mile west of Emsworth.

Wodehouse offered Westbrook occasional 'stand-in' work on the 'By The Way' column of *The Globe*. Westbrook was tall, good-looking, and had a very high opinion of himself. He was charming to women but saw no reason to work particularly hard at anything. He contributed to various magazines, wrote a few theatrical sketches with

Wodehouse and was co-author of *The Globe By The Way Book* and *Not George Washington*, where he is clearly drawn as Julian Eversleigh and Wodehouse is drawn as James Cloyster.

In 1905 a school friend of Wodehouse's, Bill Townend, told him of the adventures of an acquaintance who had tried to run a chicken farm in Devonshire with a complete ignorance of chickens but a boundless confidence in his ability to make it a profitable concern. After a few weeks the whole affair had come to a chaotic conclusion with a crowd of furious creditors descending on the establishment. Wodehouse developed the anecdote into his first adult novel, *Love Among the Chickens* (1906), and made Stanley Featherstonehaugh (pronounced Fanshaw) Ukridge the main protagonist.

In 1912 Westbrook married Ella King-Hall, sister of Baldwin King-Hall, and Wodehouse, who liked Ella, made her his UK literary agent. She was the breadwinner in the marriage, since Westbrook appears to have done little after this, other than writing two books and some magazine articles.

It is not known exactly how long Westbrook worked on *The Globe* column, but it was perhaps until 1912, and it is clear that Wodehouse had come to see through his pretensions by then, but was reluctant to ditch his friend. After 1914 they did not meet again until 1923, when Wodehouse wrote to Bill Townend:

> Out of the blue, old Brook wants to get in touch. He gives me the heeby-jeebies.

Wodehouse and Westbrook lunched together, and their meeting had a surprising result. Meeting someone after some years or revisiting a place he had once known well seems to have inspired Wodehouse to write stories about them. In this case, he must have realised the similarity between Westbrook and the Stanley Ukridge of *Love Among the Chickens*. The result was *Ukridge* (1924), featuring Ukridge in a series of money-making projects that always ended in disaster.

Impetuous, unwilling to settle down to regular employment and convinced he was always right, Ukridge sponged off his friends, stealing their tobacco, clothes and personal belongings without compunction. He ignored their reproaches, urging them to adopt 'the big, broad flexible outlook' when he 'borrowed' their top hat or new lounge suit.

Herbert Wotton Westbrook.

> *I resent these slurs, Corky. Whenever I have had occasion to pinch anything from my aunt, it has always been from the most scrupulous motives, with the object of collecting a little ready cash in order to lay the foundations of a vast fortune. ('The Level Business Head')*

Ukridge's feats include stealing his aunt's Pekinese dogs to train for a stage dog act, managing a heavyweight boxer who is reluctant to fight, seeking to make a good impression on his fiancée's aunt by stealing her beloved parrot so he can 'rescue' it later and, when left in charge of his aunt's house, turning it into an illegal gambling den.

Far-fetched? Certainly, but we do know that Herbert Westbrook took a cavalier view of other people's property and, at least once, borrowed Wodehouse's evening dress suit without bothering to ask him. This meant Wodehouse had to attend a smart dinner party in an uncle's suit which was much too big for him. To confirm the resemblance, when Wodehouse bought a banjo, it is reported that Westbrook 'borrowed' it, pawned it – and then lost the pawn ticket.

Then I fraternized with a man called Westbrook, and it is he who really is Ukridge. We shared rooms together (for which I always had to pay!) and roamed London together from 1903 to 1914. (Wodehouse letter, 28 March 1958)

· 5 ·

NEW YORK AND MARRIAGE

IN 1904 WODEHOUSE PAID a short visit to New York. He had always been fascinated by American phraseology ('Americanisms'), and his stay there included meeting the champion boxer Kid McCoy, which led to a series of stories about an American pugilist named Kid Brady.

In 1909 he paid another visit to New York and sold two short stories for $500 – much more than he would have received in London. He promptly resigned from *The Globe* and took a room in Hotel Earle, now named Washington Square Hotel, which would also feature in his stories ('In Alcala' and *The Small Bachelor*). This trip led to *Psmith, Journalist*, featuring corrupt tenement landlords and New York gangs. Bat Jarvis is an accurate portrayal of the notorious gang leader Monk Eastman.

In a few months, however, Wodehouse's initial success faded, so he returned to London and rejoined *The Globe*. It was the beginning of a habit he was to follow for the next twenty years. As he said: 'I sort of shuttled to and fro across the Atlantic.' *The Girl on the Boat* and especially *The Luck of the Bodkins* reflect these frequent voyages.

In 1910 he was back in New York when the impresario William Brady wanted to turn his novel *A Gentleman of Leisure* into a play; because of delays in the casting, he returned again in 1911. The play opened on Broadway on 24 August 1911 with Douglas Fairbanks playing the lead. By then Wodehouse was once more in London and playing cricket for the Authors v. Publishers at Lord's under the captaincy of Conan Doyle. (When the same play, renamed *A Thief for a Night*, opened in Chicago in 1913, John Barrymore played the lead.)

On 2 August 1914, Wodehouse arrived in New York again. The following day a friend, Norman Thwaites, invited him to join a double date with Thwaites' girlfriend and another girl. The other girl was the widowed Ethel Wayman, who was visiting New York with a touring repertory company. Within two months of their meeting, she and Wodehouse were married at the Church of

> *When you marry, Sally, grab a chump. Tap his forehead first, and if it rings solid, don't hesitate. All the unhappy marriages come from the husband having brains. What good are brains to a man? They only unsettle him. (The Adventures of Sally)*

the Transfiguration (the Little Church Around the Corner) on 29th Street. They had a two-night honeymoon in the Astor Hotel and then rented a house at Bellport on the south shore of Long Island. (The house features in *Jill the Reckless* and *The Adventures of Sally*.)

Wodehouse biographer Robert McCrum believes that Wodehouse and Ethel realised they needed each other. Both had had a solitary childhood, and after being widowed twice, she needed him for the security he afforded. He needed her to organise his life and give him a stable setting in which to work. Through their years together, he would write her loving notes telling her how lucky he was to have married her.

In many ways it was a marriage based on the attraction of opposites. Wodehouse was quiet and disliked parties; Ethel was talkative and loved company.

He was never happier than when absorbed in his writing; she liked meeting people. He was extremely careful with money; she was extravagant. Yet they remained a happy and devoted couple for more than sixty years. He also acquired a stepdaughter, Ethel's daughter Leonora, whom he adopted and who would become a beloved confidante and companion.

The Wodehouses – Leonora, P.G. and Ethel – at Waterloo Station around 1930, prior to a trip to the US. (Courtesy of Sir Edward Cazalet and the Wodehouse Estate)

• IMAGES •

'She gave you beans, did she?'

'With no niggardly hand. It was an extraordinary feeling, standing there while she put me through it. One had a dazed sensation of something small and shrill whirling about one, seething with fury. Like being attacked by a Pekinese.'

'I've never been attacked by a Pekinese.'

'Well, ask the man who has.'

(Joy in the Morning)

Into the face of the young man who sat on the terrace of the Hotel Magnifique at Cannes there had crept a look of furtive shame, the shifty, hangdog look which announces that an Englishman is about to talk French.

(The Luck of the Bodkins)

She came leaping towards me, like Lady Macbeth coming to get first-hand news from the guest room.

(Joy in the Morning)

He spoke with a certain what-is-it in his voice, and I could see that, if not actually disgruntled, he was far from being gruntled, so I tactfully changed the subject.

(*The Code of the Woosters*)

It was a confusion of ideas between him and one of the lions he was hunting in Kenya that had caused A. B. Spottsworth to make the obituary column. He thought the lion was dead, and the lion thought it wasn't.

(*Ring for Jeeves*)

Reggie looked like a member of the Black Hand trying to plot assassinations while hampered by a painful gumboil. His manner was dark, furtive and agitated.

(*The Luck of the Bodkins*)

'I think you're a pig,' she said.

'A pig, maybe, but a shrewd, level-headed pig.'

(*The Code of the Woosters*)

'Odd stuff, this,' said Kay, sipping. 'Probably used for taking stains out of serge suits. Still, it certainly has authority.'

(*Frozen Assets*)

When she spoke, it was with the mildness of a cushat dove addressing another cushat dove from whom it was hoping to borrow money.

(*Jeeves in the Offing*)

She melted quite perceptibly. She did not cease to look like a basilisk, but she began to look like a basilisk who has had a good lunch.

(*The Girl on the Boat*)

6

THE PRINCESS
THEATRE SHOWS

SOON AFTER HIS MARRIAGE, Wodehouse began working for the New York magazine *Vanity Fair*, for which
he became the drama critic and for which he also
wrote articles under assumed names. As drama
critic, he reviewed shows with music by Jerome
Kern, whom he had first met in 1906 when they had
worked on *The Beauty of Bath*. Sometime in 1915,
Kern introduced him to Guy Bolton; the result was
a revolution in American musical comedy.

Because he wrote nearly 100 books, Wodehouse's
achievements in the theatre are often overlooked.
He either wrote, co-wrote or adapted nineteen
plays and provided lyrics, and often the libretti, for
nearly forty musical comedies between 1905 and
1934. Alan Jay Lerner wrote later that, as a lyric

writer, Wodehouse was 'the pathfinder for Larry Hart, Cole Porter, Ira Gershwin and everyone else who followed'.

The staple feature of American musical comedy then was simply to import or imitate Austrian operettas. Wodehouse described them in the short story 'Bill the Bloodhound'. Typically, they would feature a hero who falls in love with a pretty shop girl and is disinherited by his father. The girl flees to some seaside resort and is followed by the hero. In the next scene, he, in disguise (having changed his tie), sees her in disguise (having changed her dress), and both are observed by the hero's family butler, also in disguise as a Bath-chair man. The hero's father sees them; he is also in disguise. Each of them recognises all the others, but each thinks they themselves are unrecognised. Wodehouse's depiction concludes:

> Exeunt all, hurriedly, leaving the heroine alone on the stage. It is a crisis in the heroine's life. She meets it bravely. She sings a song entitled 'My Honolulu Queen', with a chorus of Japanese girls and Bulgarian officers.

This was no exaggeration. In those days, musical comedies were rarely based on a coherent story.

> *Musical comedy is the Irish stew of drama. Anything may be put into it, with the certainty that it will improve the general effect. ('Bill the Bloodhound')*

The 'trio of musical fame': Guy Bolton, P.G. Wodehouse and Jerome Kern.

Usually, a producer would have a star under contract and would formulate something to emphasise the star's beauty, voice or comic gift. The plot was unimportant so long as it emphasised the star's role supported by a chorus of pretty girl in

exotic costumes. As late as 1931, London enjoyed
Victoria and Her Hussar, which featured a beautiful heroine, an American ambassador, a Hungarian
colonel of hussars and a Japanese girl married to the
American ambassador's brother. The scenes were
set in Siberia, Tokyo, Russia and Hungary, with the
hard-working chorus playing Japanese coolies, loyal
servants, dinner guests, Cossacks, Hungarian hussars and, inevitably, happy villagers.

Wodehouse, Bolton and Kern changed all that.
Kern wrote new enjoyable music, Bolton created
new engaging plots and Wodehouse put lyrics to
Kern's music that were as witty as W.S. Gilbert's
and, uniquely for the time, integral to the plot. Guy
Bolton said: 'I would write a scene and hand it to
Plum and next morning find half the scene gone
and its content expressed in a lyric.'

The Princess Theatre shows were wildly popular,
as exemplified by the tribute commonly attributed
to Dorothy Parker:

This is the trio of musical fame,
Bolton and Wodehouse and Kern.
Better than anyone else I can name,
Bolton and Wodehouse and Kern.
Nobody knows what on earth they've been bitten by,

All I can say is I mean to get lit and buy
Orchestra seats for the next one that's written by
Bolton and Wodehouse and Kern.

Such was their success that one of the few things
the modest Wodehouse would ever boast about was
that, in 1917, he and Bolton had five shows running
simultaneously on Broadway. His friendship with
Guy Bolton was to last sixty years, during which
they collaborated on over twenty musical comedies, four plays, two film scripts and a book. One
Wodehouse song still often heard is 'Bill', which was
dropped from *Oh, Lady! Lady!!* but appeared in *Show
Boat* in 1927.

Wodehouse always maintained that his theatre
work had been invaluable in his writing:

The more I write, the more I am convinced that the
only way to write a popular story is to split it up into
scenes, and have as little stuff between the scenes as
possible. (*Performing Flea*)

After a period living at Great Neck, Long Island, the
Wodehouses returned to the UK, but Wodehouse continued to visit New York for more theatrical work, which
included straight plays as well as musical comedies.

7

THE LIGHT NOVELS

> *From my earliest years I had always wanted to be a
> writer. It was not that I had any particular message
> for humanity. I am still plugging away and not the
> ghost of one so far, so it begins to look as though,
> unless I suddenly hit mid-season form in my eighties,
> humanity will remain a message short. (Over Seventy)*

ALTHOUGH WODEHOUSE IS BEST known today for the
sagas featuring Bertie Wooster and Jeeves and Lord
Emsworth and Blandings Castle, they are just three
of the hundreds of characters he created over his
long writing career. Some became major characters
in their own right, while others appeared in 'one-
offs' that fall into the category of light novels.

Wodehouse had one basic plot and made no apology for it. In most of his stories, boy meets girl, boy loses girl, boy gets girl, but the stories' style changed dramatically as he realised where his strengths lay. The early novels and short stories often have a serious side to them. The semi-autobiographical *Not George Washington* (1907), *A Gentleman of Leisure* (1910), *The Little Nugget* (1913), *The Man Upstairs* (1914), *Something Fresh* (1915), *Uneasy Money* (1917), *The Man with Two Left Feet* (1917), *A Damsel in Distress* (1919), *The Coming of Bill* (1920) and *Jill the Reckless* (1921) are all light romances. They have some humorous scenes, but they concentrate on the struggles of a young man to win his girl. *The Coming of Bill* and several of the short stories, such as 'In Alcala' and 'At Geisenheimer's', demonstrate how Wodehouse could write the 'serious stuff' when he wanted to.

From 1916 onwards, Wodehouse, anxious to sell his books in both America and Britain, began to write about Englishmen in love with American girls and American men falling for English girls. In *Indiscretions of Archie* (1921), we meet Archie Moffam, a Bertie Wooster lookalike whose adventures as a loving but financially incapable husband would later be matched by Bingo Little.

> *He and Rosie had always been like a couple of turtle-doves, but he knew only too well that when the conditions are right, a female turtle dove can express herself with a vigour a Caribbean hurricane might envy. ('Leave It to Algy')*

Archie Moffam (pronounced Moom) sets a pattern for us. From Archie onwards, we can be pretty certain that if a young man's name ends in 'ie' or 'y' – Reggie, Monty, Archie, Eggy, Gussie, Freddie, Bertie or Barmy – he is probably a member of the Drones Club (see Chapter 11), and the nice girl he eventually marries will have enough sense for both of them, take him in hand and make a man of him.

If he has a good, solid name – John, Joe, Mike or Bill (Wodehouse's favourite name) – then he is a young man with honourable intentions and able to provide a good home for the girl he marries, though some misunderstanding will always cause her to hate him before she at last realises his true worth.

Conversely, if a girl is named Bobbie (Wickham), Stiffy (Byng), Nobby (Hopwood) or Lottie (Blossom), then she is attractive but she is a human time bomb. She is charming, unscrupulous, quarrelsome and lovable, and her bright ideas cause chaos for all around her. If her name is Jane, Joan, Ann, Sally or Elizabeth, then she is a nice, sensible girl and probably the heroine of the story. If she is unfortunate enough to be named Gertrude, Florence, Madeline or Honoria, then she will try to mould her fiancé, make him stop smoking, force him to read improving books and probably want him to resign from the Drones Club.

> *Hypatia, like all girls who intend to be good wives, made it a practice to look upon any suggestions thrown out by her future lord and master as fatuous and futile. ('Gala Night')*

8

THE GOLF STORIES
AND MR MULLINER

> *A golfer needs a wife, true. It is essential that he
> has a sympathetic listener always handy, to whom
> he can relate the details of the day's play. ('Up from
> the Depths')*

· THE GOLF STORIES ·

IN 1922 WODEHOUSE PUBLISHED *The Clicking of
Cuthbert*, a collection of golf stories narrated by the
Oldest Member (of the golf club) which proved
to be an instant success. Because he was never an
expert at the game (his lowest handicap was probably 14), Wodehouse was able to describe perfectly
the trials and tribulations of poor golfers trying to

impress their girlfriends, as well as the pleasure (and surprise) of hitting a perfect drive or holing a long putt, and he was able to pass on these emotions to his readers.

The old names for golf clubs have vanished to be replaced by numbers, and the terms 'baffy', 'long iron', 'mashie' and 'niblick' mean little to today's players, but the stories are still enjoyed by golfers and non-golfers alike.

Many golfers still miss the old rule that, unless a ball was under water, you played where it lay. If you did not do so, you lost the hole. This gave rise to splendid real incidents of determined players climbing trees or risking their lives playing the ball from a hornet's nest. In the short story 'The Clicking of Cuthbert', a meeting of the Wood Hills Literary Society is disrupted when a golf ball comes through an open window:

[It] had come within an inch of incapacitating Raymond Parsloe Devine, the rising young novelist (who rose at that moment a clear foot and a half) from any further exercise of his art. Two inches, indeed, to the right and Raymond must inevitably have handed in his dinner-pail.

To make matters worse, a ring at the front-door bell followed almost immediately, and the maid ushered in a young man of pleasing appearance in a sweater and baggy knickerbockers who apologetically but firmly insisted on playing his ball where it lay, and what with the shock of the lecturer's narrow escape and the spectacle of the intruder standing on the table and working away with a niblick, the afternoon's session had to be classified as a complete frost.

Although Wodehouse had played the occasional game of golf before, we know that he took it up seriously in March 1918 when he and Ethel moved to Arrandale Avenue, Great Neck, Long Island.

> *'I killed him with my niblick,' said Celia.*
>
> *I nodded. If the thing was to be done at all, it was unquestionably a niblick shot. ('The Salvation of George Mackintosh')*

> *When I played, I never lost my temper. Sometimes, it is true, I may, after missing a shot, have broken my club across my knees; but I did it in a calm and judicial spirit, because the club was obviously no good and I was going to get another one anyway. ('Ordeal by Golf')*

Wodehouse gave his fictional golf club various names in English editions: Wood Hills, Woodhaven and Marvis Bay. In the American edition, *Golf Without Tears*, he called it the Manhooset Golf and Country Club, which gave his readers a slight clue since Great Neck looks onto Manhasset Bay. Not until 1966 did he use the real name. In 'Life with Freddie', we learn that Freddie Threepwood lives in Great Neck, 'near what had been the Sound View golf course till the developers took it over'.

In 1983, Walter White, a Wodehouse enthusiast, found a man who had been a caddy and member at Sound View who walked him round the housing estate now covering the old course. By comparing Wodehouse's stories to the layout of the old course, Walter confirmed that the Oldest Member's course in *The Clicking of Cuthbert* and *The Heart of a Goof* matched the Sound View course in every detail.

Tucked away among the new houses, one part of the course can still be seen. In Wodehouse's stories, poor golfers always regarded the Lake Hole with fear and trepidation, since the tee shot was over a stretch of water. The lake is still there, on the north edge of Pond Park in Great Neck, and a small bungalow now stands on what was the tee from which so many golf balls were topped into the water.

When Walter White visited England, I took him to see two courses Wodehouse had played – Walton Heath and Addington. He was keen to visit Addington, since the preface to *The Heart of a Goof* is signed 'P.G. Wodehouse, The Sixth Bunker, Addington'. As can be seen in the picture (overleaf), the bunker guarding the green at the sixth hole is some 12–15ft deep. Unless you are an extremely competent player, this bunker means trouble. No wonder Wodehouse immortalised it.

> *If you find anything in this volume that amuses you, kindly bear in mind that it was probably written on my return home after losing three balls in the gorse or breaking the head off a favourite driver. (Introduction to The Clicking of Cuthbert)*

> *Peter and James had played over the lake hole so often that they had become accustomed to it and had grown into the habit of sinking a ball or two as a preliminary formality with much the same stoicism displayed by those kings in ancient and superstitious times who used to fling jewellery into the sea to propitiate it before they took a voyage.* ('A Woman Is Only a Woman')

Wodehouse fan Walter White in the Sixth Bunker at Addington.

• MR MULLINER •

Wodehouse kept a very close eye on his market, aiming his stories at magazines like the *Saturday Evening Post* in America and *Pearson's*, *The Royal*, *The Windsor Magazine* and, above all, *The Strand* in the UK.

The Strand began in 1891 and immediately became popular by publishing Conan Doyle's Sherlock Holmes stories; its sales soon rose to over half a million and stayed at that level for nearly forty years. Wodehouse published his first story, 'The Wire-Pullers', in *The Strand* in July 1905; it featured his stories regularly for thirty-five years.

In the early twentieth century, the British Empire covered a quarter of the globe. As a result, every magazine had stories about exotic tropical places, and Wodehouse noted that they all seemed to begin the same way. The narrator would say he was 'in the club one night with the Colonel, Smithers the QC, Jack Carruthers home on leave from India and a couple of other chaps'. Someone would inquire about an absent friend in Burmah, which would prompt Jack Carruthers to say, 'did I ever tell you chaps about a dashed rum thing that happened to me in Burmah years ago?' He then narrates the story about the chap who shot the sacred crocodile or offended the local ju-ju man or whatever it was.

Wodehouse adopted the idea. His narrator was Mr Mulliner:

> ... a short, stout comfortable man of middle age and the thing that struck me first about him was the extraordinary childlike candour of his eyes. They were large, round and honest. I would have bought oil stock from him without a tremor. ('The Truth about George')

Mr Mulliner presides over the bar parlour of the Anglers' Rest beside the River Severn, where his audience comprises a variety of drinkers known to us only by their beverages; they include a Gin-and-Ginger-Ale, a Draught Stout, a tactless Mild-and-Bitter, and a flushed Lemon Squash who argues heatedly with a scowling Tankard of Ale. There is no topic of conversation that does not remind Mr Mulliner of a story concerning some relative – a niece, nephew, uncle or distant clergyman cousin.

We meet more than thirty relatives, from Adrian, Anselm and Archibald Mulliner to Lady Wilhelmina, William and Wilmot Mulliner, and every enthusiast has his favourite. Mine is that splendid curate,

> *This revelation of the character of the girl to whom he had given a curate's unspotted heart had stunned him. Myrtle, it seemed to him, appeared to him to have no notion whatsoever of the distinction between right and wrong. And while this would not have mattered, of course, had he been a gun-man and she his prospective moll, it made a great deal of difference to one who hoped later to become a vicar and, in such event, would want his wife to look after the parish funds. ('Anselm Gets His Chance')*

the Reverend Augustine Mulliner, similar to W.S. Gilbert's pale young curate, the possessor of 'flaxen hair, weak blue eyes, and the general demeanour of a saintly but timid codfish'. Under the influence of a pick-me-up, Buck-U-Uppo, concocted by his chemist uncle Wilfred, Augustine becomes a changed man. After putting his tyrannical landlady in her place, Augustine uses a well-aimed stone to see off a fierce dog chasing his bishop, leaps through a window to reprove his bad-tempered vicar and the bishop, old schoolfellows about to come to blows, and concludes by bending the bishop's terrifying wife to his will.

In later stories, under the influence of Buck-U-Uppo, the bishop is inspired to cover with pink paint a statue he is to unveil in the morning and, dressed as Sinbad the Sailor, attend a gala night at a nightclub, where he plugs a policeman in the eye.

A few years ago I learned from a distant Wodehouse cousin that something remarkably similar had happened to a clergyman uncle with whom Wodehouse spent school holidays when his parents were in Hong Kong. His uncle had not been well and a local chemist recommended his own special tonic. This apparently worked very well, and so when the local bishop arrived to preach at Evensong and said he was feeling under the weather, his uncle recommended the tonic. The bishop duly took some, as did the rector to keep him company. The tonic clearly had a high alcoholic content since the service had to be cancelled due to the inability of either rector or bishop to do more than totter and smile vaguely. The cousin recalled that Wodehouse was staying with his uncle at the time!

· 9 ·

HOLLYWOOD

IN SEPTEMBER 1929, WODEHOUSE, then in New York working on a show for Florenz Ziegfeld, decided to make a short visit to Hollywood. Some of his stories had already been filmed for the silent screen, and with the coming of sound, Hollywood needed people to write dialogue. Wodehouse had received several offers but, reluctant to commit himself until he had seen the place, he made a short trip there. This coincided with the visit of Winston Churchill, and an old friend from the Princess Theatre days, Marion Davies, smuggled him into the lunch William Randolph Hearst gave in Churchill's honour. Wodehouse's comment was typical:

> I have reluctantly come to the conclusion that I must have one of those meaningless faces which make no

impression whatsoever on the beholder. This was – I think – the seventh time I have been introduced to Churchill, and I could see that I came upon him as a complete surprise once more. (*Performing Flea*)

He signed a contract with Metro-Goldwyn-Mayer for $2,000 a week and returned to Hollywood on 8 May 1930. As he made clear later in his superb short stories satirising Hollywood, film-making was then a very confused process. With the rush to use writers to produce dialogue, the studio heads, often as autocratic as Wodehouse drew them, seemed to have come to the conclusion that if one scenario and one scriptwriter was good, then six scenario writers and six scriptwriters were better. A script went through half a dozen hands before it reached Wodehouse, after which it went through half a dozen more before the final version was accepted.

Wodehouse's first film was *Those Three French Girls*, in which some of his dialogue was used and in which, coincidentally, the cranky Earl of Ippleton was played by George Grossmith Jr, who had frequently collaborated on or performed in Wodehouse shows in London (see Chapter 15). He was then put to work on *Rosalie*, a 1928 musical comedy for which he had provided several lyrics. Two film versions had been dropped and Wodehouse was commissioned to rewrite it as a novelette suitable for filming, but this was also abandoned.

He then worked on Siegfried Geyer's play *Candle-Light*, which had been a success in London with Leslie Howard and Gertrude Lawrence and which Wodehouse had already revised for its American opening in 1929. This also was dropped, and with some minor contributions of dialogue in other films, this was about the sum total of his work in Hollywood. He failed to persuade the studio to film any of his own stories.

Wodehouse's contract ended on 9 May 1931. On 7 June, he gave an interview to the *Los Angeles Times* in which he said that he could not understand why the studio had employed him at such a large salary since they had difficulty in finding him something to do. The report caused uproar in the industry, which was already under attack for its extravagant expenditure.

Nevertheless, MGM called him back again for a six-month contract in October 1936. This time the Wodehouses took a house at 1315 Angelo Drive, which became the setting of his novel *The Old Reliable* (1951). Remembering his stories about Hollywood, it comes as no surprise that the first job he was given was a rewrite of *Rosalie*. Though taken out of his hands and revised, it was eventually released in 1937 and did very well.

After his MGM contract expired in April 1937, Wodehouse stayed in Hollywood working for other studios. Radio-Keith-Orpheum asked him to adapt his novel *A Damsel in Distress* for the screen. Fred Astaire and the then little-known Joan Fontaine played the leads; George Burns and Gracie Allen were added to emphasise the comedy. Despite this cast and a Gershwin score, the film was a flop, the first failure in Astaire's career, maybe because his public had got too accustomed to him dancing with Ginger Rogers.

In November 1937 the Wodehouses returned to their home in Le Touquet, France. His Hollywood career was over, but it resulted in brilliant satires of the film industry in the novel *Laughing Gas* (1936) and a number of Mr Mulliner short stories.

WODEHOUSE'S LONDON AND DULWICH

WODEHOUSE SAW LONDON FIRST as a schoolboy passing through it to and from Dulwich, then as a bank clerk, then as a freelance writer. His early stories depict London through the eyes of an impecunious writer – the cheap-and-cheerful London of lodgings in Chelsea, worry about the rent, and celebration dinners in Soho at half a crown (12½ pence) with a bottle of wine for a shilling (5 pence). His growing success (and his own addresses) were reflected in the later changes of setting to the London of Bertie Wooster and the Drones; of Berkeley Square and Grosvenor Square, with 'Barribault's Hotel' (Claridge's) 'just around the corner'.

He went to live in France in 1934 and saw London for the last time in July 1939. Because of this, his settings are nearly all of pre-war London, though he did try to remain up to date. He relied on Bill Townend and Guy Bolton to tell him what things were like in post-war England (see *Ring for Jeeves*), and the opening paragraph of Chapter 4 of *Bachelors Anonymous* is an accurate picture of how girls like Sally Fitch lived in London in the 1960s.

In his early days, Wodehouse had lodgings in various parts of London, and after he married, his frequent trips to America meant he and Ethel rented houses for short periods. He lived at fourteen London addresses between 1900 and 1934 and most of them appear in his stories. They include:

- Prince of Wales Mansions, Battersea. In 1913 Wodehouse shared a flat with Charles Bovill. (See *Bill the Conqueror* and 'The Romance of an Ugly Policeman'.)

- 18 Berkeley Street. The Wodehouses lived here in 1922. (See 'Sir Roderick Comes to Lunch'.)

- 47 Charles Street. Ian Hay lived here in 1926, and Wodehouse worked with him on three plays. This address became the residence of Aunt Dahlia in *The Code of the Woosters* and *Jeeves and the Feudal Spirit*.

- 17 Norfolk Street (now Dunraven Street). The Wodehouses lived here from 1927 to 1934; the blue plaque on the house was unveiled by Her Majesty the Queen Mother in 1988. This was Lord Emsworth's London residence in *Summer Lightning*.

- Dulwich, where Wodehouse went to school, also appeared in his stories in the guise of the idyllic suburb 'Valley Fields'. When his parents returned

The blue plaque on the house at 17 Dunraven Street (formerly Norfolk Street), the Wodehouses' residence from 1927 to 1934.

from Hong Kong in 1896, they rented a house at 62 Croxted Road (now rebuilt). Wodehouse renamed it as 'Mon Repos, Burberry Road'; 'Restharrow, Croxley Road'; and 'The Laurels, Burbage Road'. (See *Sam the Sudden*; *Pearls, Girls and Monty Bodkin*; *Bachelors Anonymous*.)

- On his frequent trips back to Dulwich later to watch school matches, Wodehouse walked down Acacia Grove to the Alleyn's Head pub to have lunch. It appears under its own name in *Psmith in the City*, but it is better known as 'Mulberry Grove', where 'Peacehaven' and 'Castlewood' are home to many characters in the stories. The sphinxes by the front door of 'Peacehaven' are still to be seen on the right as you enter Acacia Grove. (See *Big Money*, *Something Fishy*, *Ice in the Bedroom*.)

She looked like something that might have occurred
to Ibsen in one of his less frivolous moments.

(*Summer Lightning*)

In order to make a song a smash it is not enough for
the singer to be on top of his form. The accompanist, also, must do his bit. And the primary thing a
singer expects from his accompanist is that he shall
play the accompaniment of the song he is singing.

('The Masked Troubadour')

His reputation is that of a man who, if there are
beans to be spilled, will spill them with a firm
and steady hand. He has never kept a secret and
never will. His mother was frightened by a BBC
announcer.

(*Spring Fever*)

Any male turtle dove will tell you that, if conditions are right, the female turtle dove can spit on her hands and throw her weight about like Donald Duck.

('The Editor Regrets')

He liked his curates substantial, and Bill proved definitely the large economy size, the sort of curate whom one could picture giving the local back-slider the choice between seeing the light or getting plugged in the eye.

(*Service with a Smile*)

"The voice of Love seemed to call to me, but it was a wrong number."

('The Spot of Art')

"There are moments, Jeeves, when one asks one-self, 'Do trousers matter?'"
"The mood will pass, sir."

(*The Code of the Woosters*)

A spasm of Napoleonic strategy seized Sam. He dropped silently to the floor and concealed himself under the desk. Napoleon was always doing that sort of thing.

(*The Girl on the Boat*)

Love is a delicate plant that needs constant tending and nurturing, and this cannot be done by snorting at the adored object like a gas explosion and calling her friends lice.

(*Jeeves and the Feudal Spirit*)

"You can't go by what a girl says when she's giving you the devil for making a chump of yourself. It's like Shakespeare. Sounds well, but doesn't mean anything."

(*Joy in the Morning*)

· 11 ·

CLUBS

WHILE EVERYONE REMEMBERS THE immortal Drones Club, it is only one of many clubs in Wodehouse's stories. Although he was happy to mention real ones – the Athenaeum, Bachelors', Constitutional and others – he created his own, which included the Barrel Club, Junior Ganymede, Junior Lipstick, Senior Conservative and United Explorers.

Wodehouse began writing during the heyday of clubs. Servants were still cheap, property was easy to rent and there were plenty of people with the money and leisure time to make clubs an important element of London society. There were no fewer than 140 clubs in the West End, including twelve for ladies.

Although he often changed the real names, it is usually easy to identify which club Wodehouse had in mind. The Antiquarian, the Demosthenes and Lord Uffenham's Mausoleum Club are all based on the august Athenaeum, of which Gally Threepwood did not have a high opinion:

> He might be wronging the institution, but he doubted if it contained in its membership list a single sportsman capable of throwing soft-boiled eggs at an electric fan or smashing the piano on a Saturday night. (*Galahad at Blandings*)

In *Uneasy Money*, Lord Dawlish is secretary of a prestigious and venerable club – Brown's. It needs little imagination to identify it as London's oldest club, White's, at the top of St James's Street. And Wodehouse's helpful habit of often keeping the same initial letter when he disguised names means that we can make a pretty good guess at the two clubs who had the honour of counting Bertie Wooster's Uncle George (Lord Yaxley) among their members. We read that he was 'one of those birds in tight morning-coats and grey toppers whom you see toddling along St James's Street on fine after-noons, puffing a bit as they make the grade'. His two clubs, the Buffers and Senior Buffers, fit very well with Boodle's and Brooks's, which face each other across St James's Street.

Wodehouse was not a gregarious man, and his preference was for clubs where he could get a good meal and with a decent library where he could work in peace. Although he was a member of one lively Bohemian club, the Yorick, in his early years, and joined the Garrick, Savage and Beefsteak later, as well as the Coffee House and Lotos in New York, he did not stay with them long. One club to which he did remain faithful for many years was the institution he drew as the Senior Conservative.

• THE SENIOR CONSERVATIVE CLUB •

This club appears in nine Wodehouse stories; its members include Rupert Psmith, Mr Bickersdyke, Lord Emsworth, Jimmy Crocker and J.G. Butterwick. In *Psmith in the City*, we learn it was celebrated for the steadfastness of its political views, the excellence of its cuisine, and the curiously Gorgonzola-esque marble of its main staircase:

The Earl of Emsworth stood in the doorway of the Senior Conservative Club's vast dining-room, and beamed with a vague sweetness upon the two hundred or so Senior Conservatives, who, with much clattering of knife and fork, were keeping body and soul together by means of the coffee-room luncheon ...

Nobody appeared to notice him. He so seldom came to London these days that he was practically a stranger in the club; and in any case your Senior Conservative, when at lunch, has little leisure for observing anything not immediately on the table in front of him. To attract attention in the dining-room of the Senior Conservative Club between the hours of one and two-thirty, you have to be a mutton chop, not an earl. (*Something Fresh*)

The Senior Conservative stands in Northumberland Avenue off Trafalgar Square. Its real-life model was the Constitutional Club, which, from 1883 to 1960, stood a few yards down Northumberland Avenue on the left. Wodehouse joined it soon after he came to London and remained a member because it was large, quiet and impersonal, exactly what he wanted – a place where he could escape from his wife Ethel's busy social life and where nobody would dream of disturbing him as he worked in the library.

It is probable that, apart from giving him a 'respectable club' setting when he needed one, the

Constitutional gave Wodehouse the inspiration for the plot of *Psmith in the City*. That novel revolves around the struggle between Psmith, a junior clerk in the New Asiatic Bank, and the bank manager, Mr Bickersdyke. Since both are members of the Senior Conservative, Psmith is able to shadow Mr Bickersdyke in his leisure hours, to the latter's considerable annoyance. This seems an unlikely scenario until one learns that, in Wodehouse's time at the Hong Kong and Shanghai Bank, the manager of the Lombard Street office was Sir Ewen Cameron. *Who's Who* states that Sir Ewen's club was the Constitutional, the same as that of his young bank clerk, P.G. Wodehouse. Coincidence? Possibly. And by another coincidence, Sir Ewen's great-great-grandson is also a senior Conservative; he is David Cameron, MP.

• THE JUNIOR GANYMEDE •

At the other end of the social scale is Jeeves' club, the Junior Ganymede. Every Wodehouse enthusiast knows of the famous club book in which members are compelled to enter the personal habits and idiosyncrasies of their employers. We enter its premises only once, in *Much Obliged, Jeeves*, which was published on Wodehouse's 90th birthday in 1971.

In that story Bertie, stumbling in the road, is about to be hit by a passing taxi when Jeeves grabs him in time. The incident happened in Curzon Street, the address Wodehouse initially gave the club, but Jeeves takes Bertie to his club 'just around the corner' to recover. Bertie says it 'lacked the sprightliness of the Drones' but this is only natural 'when you reflected that the membership consisted of elderly butlers and gentlemen's gentlemen of fairly ripe years, but as regards comfort it couldn't be faulted'. Was there ever an institution like the Junior Ganymede?

'Just around the corner' from the eastern end of Curzon Street is Charles Street; 30 yards along Charles Street is a pub now named The Only Running Footman. Although the present building dates from the 1930s, a pub by that name has been here since the estate was built in the 1740s.

This is the heart of Mayfair, the smartest area of London, so it is odd to find small pubs scattered around it. But the developers who built Mayfair put them here for a very good reason. These houses might have had a family of three or four, but they also would have had half a dozen servants. A pub on each corner meant there was somewhere for your male servants to relax nearby rather than wandering all over London.

In the 1920s, E.V. Lucas wrote an article on 'The Club'. He had heard a rumour of a pub just off Berkeley Square which was the gathering place for the menservants of Mayfair. He went along to The Only Running Footman and talked to the landlord, learning that the rumour was true. The Private Bar was restricted to house stewards, butlers, gentlemen's personal gentlemen and valets; the Snug was for senior footmen, head grooms and the like, while the Saloon and Public Bars were for those further down the social scale. But how did Wodehouse know of it?

He knew because directly across the road is 47 Charles Street. In the 1920s, this was the home of the writer Ian Hay, where Wodehouse came often for nearly two years while they worked on three plays (*A Damsel in Distress*; *Baa, Baa, Black Sheep* and *Leave It to Psmith*). And verification came many years later from the valet of Lord Mildmay, who lived around the corner in Berkeley Square; he confirmed that the pub had indeed been the meeting place for the menservants of Mayfair. Not a clubhouse as such and no club book that I know of – but it gave Wodehouse the idea.

• THE DRONES CLUB •

The Drones Club, Dover Street, is arguably the best-loved London club in fiction. Wodehouse originally created it as an alternative fictional venue to the well-known real Bachelors' Club (founded 1881, closed 1940s), which stood down at the west end of Piccadilly.

In the same way that the bar parlour of the Anglers' Rest was used to introduce stories about Mr Mulliner's extended family, Wodehouse used the Drones' bar to introduce stories about its members. A story often opens with a Bean and an Egg grumbling at the irrational behaviour of, say, Bingo Little or Freddie Widgeon; a well-informed Crumpet will join them, reassure them there is a good reason for Bingo's or Freddie's conduct, and go on to tell us what happened.

The Drones first appears in *Jill the Reckless* (1920) when Algy Martyn gives Freddie Rooke dinner there. Since Freddie is a member of another club, the Bachelors', he has to await Algy's arrival until he can get a much-needed drink. Freddie's agony gives Wodehouse the chance to tell us:

There he sat, surrounded by happy, laughing young men, each grasping a glass of the good old mixture-as-before, absolutely unable to connect …

No wonder Freddie experienced the sort of abysmal soul-sadness which afflicts one of Tolstoi's Russian peasants when, after putting in a heavy day's work strangling his father, beating his wife, and dropping the baby into the city reservoir, he turns to the cupboard, only to find the vodka-bottle empty. (*Jill the Reckless*)

In *Leave It to Psmith* (1923) we learn the club is in Dover Street, and in *Very Good, Jeeves* (1930) we read that it possesses a swimming pool. We never see the pool, but every aficionado knows it is the source of a long-standing grudge between Bertie Wooster and Tuppy Glossop. Bertie recounts the incident in a single superb sentence:

He was the fellow, if you remember, who, ignoring a lifelong friendship in the course of which he had frequently eaten my bread and salt, betted me one night at the Drones that I wouldn't swing myself across the swimming-bath by the ropes and rings and then, with almost inconceivable treachery, went and looped back the last ring, causing me to drop into the fluid and ruin one of the nattiest suits of dress-clothes in London. ('The Ordeal of Young Tuppy')

Wodehouse named over fifty Drones members, and some became leading characters in their own right. In *Young Men in Spats* (1936) we are introduced to Freddie Widgeon, who appears in six books, Pongo Twistleton-Twistleton (five books) and Barmy Fotheringay-Phipps. The Drones Club is another small Wodehouse world where we can laugh at the misadventures of young men trying to win the girl they love. Or, in Bingo Little's case, his efforts to regain the ten pounds his wife, Rosie, gave him to put in little Algy's wee bank account and which, of course, he promptly loses betting that little Algy is the ugliest baby in Wimbledon.

Look at his story from whatever angle you pleased, it remained one that reflected little credit on a young father and at the best must inevitably lead to 'Oh, how could you?' And the whole wheeze of married life, he had come to learn, was to give the opposite number as few opportunities of saying 'Oh, how could you?' as possible. ('Sonny Boy')

Wodehouse probably put the club in Dover Street because No. 34 was home to the Bath Club. This building, destroyed during the war, had a swimming pool on the ground floor with ropes and rings above it, exactly as Bertie tells us. Wodehouse was never a member but he would certainly have known that the dastardly trick Tuppy Glossop played on Bertie was not uncommon. I was lucky enough to meet an old gentleman who had suffered exactly this indignity while wearing his first Savile Row suit.

In *The Inimitable Jeeves* (1923), Wodehouse revealed the major source of the Drones. In 'The Pride of the Woosters is Wounded', Bingo Little tells Bertie of his love for Honoria Glossop in 'the oyster bar at Buck's'. Bertie wishes he would lower his voice because 'Fred Thompson and one or two fellows had come in, and McGarry, the chappie behind the bar, was listening with his ears flapping'.

This is another example of a Wodehouse private joke. Buck's Club, still going strong at 18 Clifford Street, was founded by Herbert Buckmaster in 1919 and soon became *the* London club for young men. Fred Thompson (1884–1949), a friend of Wodehouse's and an early member of Buck's, was a well-known librettist whose successes included *The Bing Boys Are Here* (1916) and *Lady, Be Good!* (1924).

'He then gave a hideous laugh and added that, if anybody was interested in his plans, he was going to join the Foreign Legion, that Cohort of the Damned in which broken men may toil and die and, dying, forget.'

'Beau Widgeon?' said the Egg, impressed. 'What ho!'

A Crumpet shook his head.

'You won't catch Freddie joining any Foreign Legion, once he gets on to the fact that it means missing his morning cup of tea. All the same, I can understand his feeling a bit upset at the moment, poor blighter. Tragedy has come into his life. He's just lost the only girl in the world.'

'Well, he ought to be used to that by this time.'

('Noblesse Oblige')

He and Wodehouse worked together on *The Golden Moth* (1921). And McGarry, 'the chappie behind the bar', was indeed the barman at Buck's Club from 1919 to 1941.

Wodehouse was never a member of Buck's, but his son-in-law, Peter Cazalet, was. In 1933 Wodehouse's friend and colleague Guy Bolton was elected, and we know from their correspondence that he and Wodehouse lunched there frequently.

Towards the end of his life, Wodehouse was asked if the Drones was based on Buck's. He was surprised by the question since he assumed everybody knew it was. He had not realised that what was obvious to his readers in the 1930s had become myth and legend by the 1970s, but he was at pains to emphasise that the swimming-pool story was based on the Bath Club in Dover Street.

12

WODEHOUSE'S ENGLAND

WE HAVE ALREADY SEEN how Wodehouse used places where he lived in his books, whether it was changing a name (Dulwich to 'Valley Fields', Dulwich College to 'Wrykyn', Stansted Park to 'Sanstead House') or providing names for his characters (Lord Emsworth and the Threepwood family). This chapter looks at other locations in England that he used in his stories.

Wodehouse's stepdaughter, Leonora, married Peter Cazalet in 1932, and they lived at Fairlawne, Shipbourne, in Kent. Wodehouse renamed it 'Shipley Hall' in *Money in the Bank* (1942) and *Something Fishy* (1957), while Hever Castle, a few miles to the west, bears a close resemblance to 'Beevor Castle' of *Spring Fever* (1948). Further south, Emsworth became 'Belpher' in *A Damsel in Distress*, while 'Bingley-on-Sea' and 'Bramley-on-Sea' are both Wodehouse's version of Bexhill-on-Sea. The first mention of this seaside resort is in *The Girl on the Boat*, published in 1922, the year Wodehouse's parents moved from Cheltenham to Bexhill.

• WORCESTERSHIRE •

Wodehouse had several relatives in Worcestershire, including an uncle and aunt at Malvern. He often spent school holidays in the 1880s and '90s with another uncle, the Rev. Edward Isaac, rector of Hanley Castle, a small hamlet north of Upton-on-Severn, Worcestershire. Just a few miles away is Malvern College, where a housemaster, the Rev. Henry Foster, had seven sons, all of whom played cricket for the county. They inspired Wodehouse to write *Mike* (1909) – and the description of the Wrykyn playing fields in that book fits Malvern in every particular.

He does not seem to have visited the county again until 1926, when he returned to the area to take the waters at Droitwich, staying at the Chateau Impney Hotel (a remarkable building that fits exactly the description we are given of Walsingford Hall in *Summer Moonshine*). He hired a car and visited his old

Severn End in Hanley Castle, Worcestershire: the original of
Brinkley Court.

haunts, which seemed to have revived many memories. It was after this that Wodehouse began writing
of Mr Mulliner, who told his stories at the Anglers'
Rest, and created Aunt Dahlia's country residence –
Brinkley Court, Worcestershire.

The Anglers' Rest is almost certainly The King's
Head, beside the river in Upton-on-Severn, while
Brinkley Court bears a remarkable resemblance to
Severn End, the ancestral home of the Lechmere
family, in Hanley Castle (a mile north of Upton). As a
boy, Wodehouse had often stayed at Hanley Castle with
his uncle, the Rev. Mr Isaac, and his memories of that
time probably inspired Mr Mulliner's stories about his

clerical relations (see 'Mulliner's Buck-U-Uppo').
The area also provided the setting for one of his classic
short stories, 'The Great Sermon Handicap'.

Although a small hamlet, Hanley Castle has an
ancient grammar school. Wodehouse used it as
the setting for one of his funniest scenes – Gussie
Fink-Nottle's presentation of the prizes at Market
Snodsbury Grammar School in *Right Ho, Jeeves*.
Wodehouse used the name Market Snodsbury for
Upton-on-Severn/Hanley Castle because nearby
lies a small village with a name he never forgot:
Upton Snodsbury, the only Snodsbury place name
in England.

> *'Well, you know how many parsons there are round
> about here. There are about a dozen hamlets within a
> radius of six miles, and each hamlet has a church and
> each church has a parson and each parson preaches
> a sermon every Sunday. Tomorrow week – Sunday the
> twenty-third – we're running off the Great Sermon
> Handicap. Steggles is making the book. Each parson
> is to be clocked by a reliable clerk of the course, and
> the one that preaches the longest sermon wins.' ('The
> Great Sermon Handicap')*

We read of Lesser-Snodsbury-in-the-Vale, Worcestershire, in 'The Truth About George', and Lower Snodsbury is mentioned in *Ring for Jeeves*. Upton Snodsbury appears under its real name in 'The Luck of the Stiffhams' as well as in *Money for Nothing*.

• NORFOLK •

Although Wodehouse had visited many large country houses, either accompanying his aunts in Wiltshire and, later, his parents in Shropshire, he had always done so as a visitor, for lunch or dinner. Christmas 1924, however, saw him and his wife staying at a historic house he came to know very well indeed – Hunstanton Hall in north Norfolk.

Wodehouse loved the place from the moment he saw it. Over the next ten years, he and Ethel were regular guests of the owner, Charles le Strange, and in 1933 they rented the house for some months. The ancestral home of the le Strange family for centuries, it was as near to living at Blandings as Wodehouse ever got. It showed him what life was like in a great house and gave him an invaluable insight into the problems facing landowners in the twentieth century. In a letter to Bill Townend (12 May 1929), he wrote:

It is one of those enormous houses, two thirds of which are derelict … [I]t's happening all over the country now – thousands of acres, park, gardens, moat etc and priceless heirlooms but not a penny of ready money.

Hunstanton's influence in Wodehouse's stories was almost immediate. In *Money for Nothing*, the hall, moat and grounds are based so closely on Hunstanton that he had to disguise it by 'moving' it across country to Worcestershire. The moat surrounding the

Hunstanton Hall, Norfolk. (Courtesy of Karen Shotting)

house was extended to form a lake on one side, and Wodehouse used to spend his mornings working in a punt moored to the bank. When the punt was refurbished, Charles le Strange had the name 'Plum' painted on it to commemorate his usage.

In 'Jeeves and the Impending Doom', Bertie's cousin, the abominable Thos, maroons Cabinet Minister Mr Filmer on a small island in the middle of a lake. Rain is pouring down when Bertie sets off with Jeeves to rescue Filmer. They find him shouting for help from the top of a small building which he has climbed to escape an angry swan. Bertie tells us the edifice is known as the Octagon:

> This building was run up somewhere in the last century, I have been told, to enable the grandfather of the late owner to have some quiet place out of earshot of the house where he could practise the fiddle.

Also attacked by the swan, Bertie emulates Filmer by climbing onto the roof:

> Whoever built the Octagon might have constructed it especially for this sort of crisis. Its walls had grooves at regular intervals which were just right for the hands and feet.

Tamaki Morimura scales the Octagon at Hunstanton, as Bertie Wooster did in 'Jeeves and the Impending Doom'.

The Octagon – which was indeed built by Sir Hamon le Strange around 1640, as a place where he could practise the viol out of his wife's hearing – still exists. In 2011 it was visited by members of The P.G. Wodehouse Society (UK), who naturally had to try out Bertie's route to the top.

Hunstanton also gave Wodehouse the source of a major Blandings character, but that is covered in Chapter 14.

13

THE WAR AND THE
BERLIN BROADCASTS

In June 1939, Wodehouse came over to England
from France to receive an honorary doctorate of literature from Oxford University, the first humorous
writer to receive such an honour since Mark Twain
in 1907. Some days later, he and his old friend Bill
Townend went down to watch a cricket match at
Dulwich. It was the last time he would see Townend
or his old school. On 3 September, Britain went to
war with Germany.

The Wodehouses were then living in Le Touquet,
part of a large British colony. Along with most of
their compatriots, they stayed where they were
during the 'phoney war', in the belief that British
consular officials would warn them in time to leave.
With the sudden, rapid advance of the Germans

'Plum' visiting Dulwich College sometime in the
1930s. (With kind permission of the Governors of
Dulwich College)

through northern France in 1940, the warning never came. When they did try to escape, their car broke down. After its repair, they set off again with another family, but when that family's car broke down, the Wodehouses came back to look for them. They all decided to return home and try again the next day. The following morning, 22 May 1940, the Germans arrived. Wodehouse was among those British men under 60 taken prisoner and, after being sent to Loos and then Liège, interned in a former lunatic asylum at Tost in Upper Silesia.

Wodehouse never stopped writing, even while interned, and he kept a diary which he adapted into a series of entertaining talks for his fellow internees. The talks were Wodehouse at his best: he made light of the discomfort, the cold, and the continual hunger, and he poked gentle fun at their German captors. When he was unexpectedly released three-

> *Tost is no beauty spot. It lies in the heart of sugar-beet country ... There is a flat dullness about the countryside which has led many a visitor to say, 'If this is Upper Silesia, what must Lower Silesia be like?' (Performing Flea)*

and-a-half months before his 60th birthday in 1941, he was met by two Germans whom he had known in Hollywood (one of whom was now working for the German Foreign Office). They suggested that he broadcast his experiences to friends and fans in America, then still a neutral country, to reassure them he was all right. Unaware that the Germans were using him as a pawn, and, because of his internment, ignorant of the battering Britain was then undergoing, he recorded five talks (all based on his camp talks). Though they were intended only for American listeners, they were nonetheless heard in England – where all hell broke loose.

Wodehouse was trying to show that he and his fellows were bearing up under adverse conditions, but he made their Germans guards look human, even funny. Though laudable, this did not go down well in Britain, then being bombed every night by the Luftwaffe. The result was that Duff Cooper, Minister for Information, ordered the BBC to let a journalist, William Connor, broadcast a vitupera-tive attack on Wodehouse on 15 July 1941. The BBC protested it was completely unjustified and highly libellous, but Duff Cooper overruled them. Most of the subsequent letters they received criticised not Wodehouse but the BBC for allowing Connor's talk. This forced Duff Cooper to state publicly that he was responsible, but the damage had been done.

While it is believed fewer than 100 people in the UK heard the Wodehouse talks, half the country seems to have heard – and remembered – Connor's appalling attack. (Years later, Connor realised Wodehouse was innocent and made him a full and generous apology.)

In 1944 the Wodehouses were in Paris when it was liberated, and Wodehouse was interrogated by Major Edward Cussen of MI5. After a thorough investigation, Cussen stated that Wodehouse had been stupid but not guilty of any crime. This was a relief to the Wodehouses, but it was more than offset by the dreadful news that their beloved daughter, Leonora, had died in hospital earlier that year. They never really recovered from this sad loss.

When the war in Europe finished in May 1945, the Wodehouses stayed in Paris. Their house in Le Touquet had been badly damaged, making it uninhabitable. After much delay, on 18 April 1947 they sailed on the *SS America* to the USA, where they remained for the rest of their lives.

The Berlin broadcasts cast a long shadow over the last thirty years of Wodehouse's life. He always regretted them and freely admitted he had been

abysmally stupid. Yet despite his complete exon-
eration, even today many people believe that
Wodehouse 'broadcast for the Germans', despite it
being due to circumstances outside his control.

Although it was announced in Parliament in
1944 that the Director of Public Prosecutions had
decided there was not sufficient evidence to pros-
ecute Wodehouse, the authorities refused to declare
him innocent – but nobody would say why. Major
Cussen went on to find more facts and evidence
exonerating him, yet as late as 1952 the Home
Secretary said he could not give an assurance that
Wodehouse would not be prosecuted if he returned
to England; that assurance was not given until the
1960s. Not until 1980 did the late Iain Sproat, MP,
manage to unearth the information that the British
Government had decided that Wodehouse was not
guilty of any crime. But because the file on him
mentioned another suspect, it had been kept secret
for thirty-five years.

Subsequent post-war investigations of German
documents showed that, as they had claimed, the
Wodehouses had received no financial assistance
or payment from the Germans and the so-called
'payments' made to him by the German Foreign
Office were royalties from Spain and other neutral

countries which had to be processed through official channels. In an answer to a later MI5 inquiry, a British Foreign Office official summed up the whole sad business: 'I do not think that anyone would seriously deny that "L'affaire Wodehouse" was very much a storm in a teacup. It is perfectly plain to any unbiased observer that Mr Wodehouse made the celebrated broadcasts in all innocence and without any evil intent.'

A full account as well as transcripts of the broadcasts can be found at: www.pgwodehousesociety.org.uk

14

BLANDINGS CASTLE, THE THREEPWOOD FAMILY AND THE EMPRESS

BLANDINGS CASTLE HAS JOINED Narnia, Brideshead and 221B Baker Street as a hallowed setting of English literature. Every enthusiast knows its rose garden, the terraces overlooking the lake, the steps down to the lawn where Gally sips a thoughtful whisky, the gardens presided over by McAllister, the cottage in the West Wood suitable for concealing diamond necklaces or Berkshire pigs, and the hamlet of Blandings Parva which adjoins the estate.

We know its residents, members of the ancient Threepwood family, equally well. We know the kindly if muddle-headed Lord Emsworth, unforgettably described as having 'one of those minds capable of accommodating but one idea at a time

— if that'. We know his younger son, Freddie, the cause of so much anguish to his father:

Years before, when a boy, and romantic as most boys are, his lordship had sometimes regretted that the Emsworths, though an ancient clan, did not possess a Family Curse. How little he had suspected that he was shortly to become the father of it. ('Lord Emsworth Acts for the Best')

We know Lord Emsworth's sisters, of whom, according to the last count (*Sunset at Blandings*), there are no fewer than ten. We meet Lady Ann Warblington in *Something Fresh*, Lady Hermione Wedge in *Full Moon* and Lady Julia Fish in *Summer Lightning*, but the one we all remember is Lady Constance Keeble (later Schoonmaker). She leads her sisters in what she sees as her duty to stop her nieces and nephews marrying badly and will bully her brother unmercifully to ensure he does not release the trust funds that would let the marriage take place. The young men in the stories fear her wrath:

'Ronnie Fish says Aunt Constance has to be seen to be believed. Hugo Carmody paled beneath his tan when he spoke of her. Monty Bodkin strongly suspects that she conducts human sacrifices at the time of the full moon.'

'Nonsense. These boys exaggerate so. Probably a gentle sweet-faced lady of the old school with mittens.' (*Uncle Fred in the Springtime*)

Lady Constance may have too rigid an attitude so far as marriages in the Threepwood clan are concerned, but one can sympathise with her to some extent:

'You mean he's an impostor?'

Lady Constance spoke with a wealth of emotion. In the past few years Blandings Castle had been peculiarly rich in impostors, notable among them Lord Ickenham and his nephew Pongo, and she had reached saturation point as regarded them, never wanting to see another as long as she lived. A hostess gets annoyed and frets when she finds that every second guest whom she entertains is enjoying her hospitality under a false name, and it sometimes seemed to her that Blandings Castle had impostors the way other houses had mice, a circumstance at which her proud spirit rebelled. (*Service with a Smile*)

And then there is Lord Emsworth's younger brother, the splendid Hon. Galahad Threepwood, who sees it as his duty to counter his sisters' attempts to thwart young love and will go to any lengths (lies, blackmail, theft) to ensure a happy ending. He is described as a 'Pink 'Un and a Pelican', which categorises him immediately as one of the men-about-town who gave the Naughty Nineties their reputation. Members of the Pelican Club (1887–92) included peers, playboys, musicians, journalists, young men with too much money and young men with no money but with all their wits about them. Their exploits in raising money by dubious means and their equally dubious methods of losing it were chronicled in the 'Pink 'Un' (*The Sporting Times*).

The 'Pink 'Un' staff, especially 'Shifter' Goldberg, were equally well known across the country for their adventures amorous and legal. Their best-known chronicler was Arthur ('Pitcher') Binstead, whose books *A Pink 'Un and a Pelican* and *Pitcher in Paradise* can still be found today. Wodehouse knew some of the 'Pink 'Un' staff from his days at *The Globe* and admired Binstead. In a letter to me, he said Binstead was a master writer and confirmed that Mustard Pott's Clothes Stakes at the Drones

Club (*Uncle Fred in the Springtime*) was a direct take-off of Binstead's account of the real Great Hat Stakes, *c.* 1900, when the first hat to come through the door of the Criterion Bar after the clock struck seven was a turban worn by a Hindu waiter bringing in an order of curry.

The younger generation of Threepwood girls are a strong-minded lot and inherit their mothers' determination when it comes to marrying the man they love. Millicent Threepwood is a typical example. She has 'soft blue eyes and a face like the Soul's Awakening. Not even an expert could have told that she had just received a whispered message from a bribed butler and was proposing at six sharp to go and meet a quite ineligible young man among the rose bushes.'

Below stairs, Sebastian Beach holds office as butler. We are familiar with his pantry and his excellent port – officially the property of Lord Emsworth, but Beach's conscience would not allow him to serve it unless he had tested it himself. We have watched him develop over the years from the pompous individual of *Something Fresh* to such an integral part of Blandings that we cannot think of it without him. An ally of the unscrupulous Galahad and the conveyor of messages between young

> *Beach the butler was a man who had made two chins grow where only one had been before, and his waistcoat swelled like the sail of a racing yacht. (Galahad at Blandings)*

lovers, he is even prepared to participate in the theft of the Empress of Blandings if it will ease the path to happiness of Ronnie Fish and Sue Brown.

And then there is McAllister. In *Something Fresh*, the head gardener is Thorne, but from *Leave It to Psmith* onwards, Angus McAllister is firmly in charge. Lord Emsworth is also a keen gardener. so naturally McAllister fights all his suggestions tooth and nail and normally prevails over the mild-mannered peer. But in 'Lord Emsworth and the Girl Friend', inspired by the heroic 12-year-old Cockney girl Gladys slipping her hand into his, the old martial spirit of the Threepwoods comes through, and Lord Emsworth defies not just McAllister but Lady Constance as well.

McAllister may be dour and unbending, but at least he gave Wodehouse the opportunity to write his often-quoted line:

It is never difficult to distinguish between a Scotsman with a grievance and a ray of sunshine. ('The Custody of the Pumpkin')

One other Blandings resident deserves mention: Lord Emsworth's pride and joy, Empress of Blandings, a Berkshire pig. In the summer of 1928, Wodehouse was staying at Hunstanton Hall and was struggling with his third Blandings novel. The first two had dealt with outsiders coming to the castle; this time, Wodehouse wanted to write a novel based on the Threepwood family. He had spent two years trying to work out a plot with no success but, at the end of this visit to Hunstanton, he wrote to a friend to say he had the answer at last. The following year *Summer Lightning* appeared, setting the pattern for Blandings novels for the next forty-five years. It introduced Gally Threepwood and established the Empress as the most important factor in Lord Emsworth's life.

A few years ago, I spoke to Mr Tom Mott, whose father had been the chauffeur at Hunstanton Hall. He remembered Wodehouse in the late 1920s and also recalled the installation of a black pig in the sty by the extensive kitchen gardens where Wodehouse used to walk. By a happy chance, he took a photograph of the

The black pig at Hunstanton Hall that inspired Wodehouse's creation of the Empress of Blandings. (Courtesy of the late Mr Tom Mott)

black pig whose arrival inspired Wodehouse to create the Empress.

In *Blandings the Blest* (1968), Geoffrey Jaggard wrote:

> As country houses go, it has a unique place in literature. It has the dominance and grandeur of the Tower of London without its grimness. To the Tower we turn our minds with a sense of history and romantic awe. To Blandings we would often be returning too, but with affection, delighted anticipation, and with an extraordinary sense of security.

It is clear Wodehouse had some stately home in mind, but the origins of Blandings have long been a matter of dispute. Wodehouse said that it was 'a mixture of places' he remembered, one of which was Corsham Court in Wiltshire. He knew it as a schoolboy, when he used to stay with his grandmother and aunts at nearby Cheney Court. But Corsham Court lies within the town and, apart from the lake in its grounds, has nothing to suggest the Blandings we know. There are many more likely candidates around Stableford, Shropshire, his family home from the age of 15 to 22. Because of the 'fake' castellations on its roof, Apley Park has been nominated by some enthusiasts, but it was built 300 years too late and possesses none of the major features of Blandings.

Weston Park, then the home of the Earl of Bradford, is almost certainly one of the places Wodehouse had in mind – but only outside the house, which is a gracious Queen Anne mansion. Within 20 miles of Stableford there is no other estate with the combined features of a drive going towards the house and then curving away from it (*Something Fresh*), where the rhododendrons hide a car after it leaves the front door (*Heavy Weather*), and where the terraces with their rose garden end at steps leading down to a lawn dominated by a splendid Cedar of Lebanon, beneath whose branches Galahad planned his strategy for foiling Constance.

Below the terraces is the lake, while to one side are the Greek temple and the woods with a secluded cottage, ideal for hiding necklaces or stolen pigs. The Shrewsbury road runs by the kitchen gardens, exactly as Wodehouse said, and the adjoining hamlet of Weston-under-Lizard fits perfectly with Blandings Parva. Every feature of the Blandings estate is to be found at Weston Park save one – the famous yew alley. That lies 70 miles to the south.

In 1902 Wodehouse's parents moved to Cheltenham, where he used to visit them. Just a few miles east of Cheltenham is Cleeve Hill, which looks down on Sudeley Castle – just as Dreever Castle was viewed from the hillside in *A Gentleman of Leisure*. Sudeley was built in the middle of the fifteenth century, as was Blandings. It has a flag tower and a ruined wing at one side, and its yew walks are famous in this part of England. In *Leave It to Psmith* we learn that Blandings is 'not ten miles from Winstone Court'. The only Winstone in England is 9 miles south of Sudeley.

Until some definite proof to the contrary comes to light, Sudeley Castle 'transplanted' to the Weston

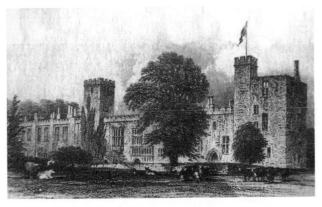

Sudeley Castle, the model for Blandings Castle. The Blandings estate was based on the grounds of Weston Park in Shropshire.

Park estate in Shropshire fulfils Wodehouse's 'mixture of places' very well indeed. The producer Verity Lambert used Sudeley as Blandings in the TV movie *Heavy Weather*, starring Peter O'Toole as Lord Emsworth and Richard Briers as Gally.

15

BERTIE WOOSTER
AND JEEVES

*It is now some fourteen summers since, an eager lad
in my early thirties, I started to write Jeeves stories:
and many people think this nuisance should now
cease. Carpers say that enough is enough. Cavillers
say the same. They look down the vista of the years and
see these chronicles multiplying like rabbits and the
prospect appals them. But against this must be set the
fact that writing Jeeves stories gives me a great deal
of pleasure and keeps me out of the public-houses.
(Preface to Very Good, Jeeves (1930))*

MY MAN JEEVES, THE first volume of Jeeves short stories and Wodehouse's twenty-third book, came out in 1919. The Jeeves stories were, with one exception, told in the first person by Bertie, straightforward and relatively easy to narrate since they involved few characters: Bertie, Jeeves, a friend in trouble and, often, an interfering aunt.

It was not until 1934 that Wodehouse published his first full-length Jeeves novel, *Thank You, Jeeves*. This was probably because, as he told his friend Bill Townend, he found the narration to be hard work. In a Blandings story, Wodehouse can tell us what is happening simultaneously at the Empress's pig sty, in the library and in Beach's pantry. But when Bertie is the narrator, the reader can only know what Bertie knows, which can be a problem in a long, complicated plot. This is one of the reasons Bertie dives behind a settee or desk so often. This is good comedy as well as enabling Wodehouse to move the plot along as Bertie overhears what other characters are saying. He did say that it got rid of the boredom of writing 'he said' and 'she said' all the time and enabled him to write 'he bawled', 'she squealed', 'he croaked' – not to mention, 'He spoke with the air of someone who has found a dead mouse in his beer: "Bertie, it's all over."'

> *It is no use telling me there are bad aunts and good aunts. At the core, they are all alike. Sooner or later, out pops the cloven hoof. (The Code of the Woosters)*

Today Bertie and Jeeves seem purely fictional characters, but that is because the world has changed so much. In 1971 Wodehouse was asked if the world he wrote about had ever really existed.

'Oh, it very definitely existed,' replied Wodehouse with animation. 'When I was living in London around the turn of the century, a good many of the young men dressed in morning coat, toppers and spats . . . Anyway, when I started writing my stories, Bertie was a recognisable type. All the rich young men had valets.'

He paused for a moment or so, then said, 'Funny how fast a type disappears! After the war, there wasn't nearly so much money around, so the young men had to go out and find jobs, and this sort of pulled the rug out from under a whole way of life. Now my stories read like historical novels.'

(*The World of P. G. Wodehouse*, Herbert Warren Wind)

• BERTIE WOOSTER •

We know a lot about Bertie, though there is still some mystery about the source of his wealth and his family antecedents. After prep school, Malvern House (the name of Wodehouse's own prep school in Dover), Bertie went on to Eton and then Oxford. Which college he attended is a matter of dispute. Was it Magdalen or Christ Church? In both *The Code of the Woosters* and *Stiff Upper Lip, Jeeves*, we are told unequivocally that Bertie was at Magdalen, but there are strong arguments for Christ Church. In *Thank You, Jeeves*, Chuffy Chufnell recalls how Bertie wanted to dive into the college fountain – and that can only be Christ Church, which, at the turn of the century, had more Etonians than all the other colleges put together.

In 1981, two Fellows of Magdalen, J.H.C. Morris and A.D. McIntyre, put forward a persuasive argument in their *Thank You, Wodehouse*. McIntyre's obituary in 1994 spoke of his excellence as a historian, his admiration for Wodehouse and his attempts 'to get one Bertram Wooster, allegedly Magdalen's most celebrated fictitious alumnus, inscribed in the college register'.

Bertie likes to lie abed of a morning but, like so many seemingly languid Edwardian young men, he is surprisingly active. He is a horseman, he shoots, and he is a keen tennis player, golfer and rackets blue. He is also a very kind-hearted young man. As the Wodehouse scholar Richard Usborne wrote, the two main commandments of the Code of the Woosters are:

(1) Thou shalt not let down a pal.
(2) Thou shalt not scorn a woman's love (no matter how much you may dislike her).

Not a bad code, but Bertie is a very likeable young man. In the introduction to the 1974 edition of *Joy in the Morning*, Wodehouse sums up Bertie and his friends perfectly:

The Edwardian knut was never an angry young man. He would get a little cross, perhaps, if his man Meadowes sent him out in the morning with odd spats on, but his normal attitude to life was sunny. He was a humble kindly soul who knew he was a silly ass but hoped you wouldn't mind. He liked everybody and most people liked him. Portrayed on the stage by George Grossmith and G.P. Huntley, he was a lovable figure, warming the hearts of all.

> You might disapprove of him not being a world's
> worker, but you could not help being fond of him.

Was there a source for Bertie, someone whom
Wodehouse had in mind? Although he used to say
that Rupert Psmith was the only character he had
had handed to him on a plate, in letters towards
the end of his life, he let more and more information slip out. The clue lies in the advice Wodehouse
gave to his friend Bill Townend: 'In writing a novel,
I always imagine I am writing for a cast of actors.'
Later, he said: 'I classed all my characters as if they
were living salaried actors.'

In the years up to 1914, Wodehouse knew lots of
young men like Bertie, but one actor fits the theory
so well, he deserves closer examination. George
Grossmith Jr (1874–1935) was the son of George
Grossmith, a leading light of Gilbert & Sullivan's
operettas. Grossmith Jr first appeared on stage in
1892 and made his name at the Gaiety Theatre playing dude parts, including Bertie Boyd in *The Shop
Girl* (1894). He went on to play dude parts for more
than thirty years.

Wodehouse probably first met Grossmith in 1907
when he was writing lyrics for the Gaiety Theatre.
Grossmith starred in Wodehouse's *Kissing Time*

George Grossmith Jr.

'Yes, sir,' said Jeeves in a low, cold voice, as if he had been bitten in the leg by a personal friend. ('Clustering Around Young Bingo')

(1919) and *Sally* (1921). They co-wrote the book and lyrics for *The Cabaret Girl* (1922) and *The Beauty Prize* (1923) and worked together again on *Those Three French Girls* (1930), Wodehouse's first film in Hollywood. Because Grossmith specialised in playing Bertie Wooster-type parts, he is an obvious choice in the development, if not the creation, of Bertie, but this was not confirmed until 1970, when Wodehouse replied to a query from a fan: 'I don't think Bertie was based on anybody, unless it was George Grossmith.'

• JEEVES •

The origins of Reginald Jeeves are less obscure. The idea of the clever servant guiding his foolish young master goes back to the ancient Greeks and was a staple factor in storytelling through the centuries right up to Pickwick's Sam Weller and Barrie's *The Admirable Crichton*. In a letter (12 January 1965), Wodehouse wrote that he had read *Ruggles of Red Gap* (1914), the American best-seller about an English valet employed by an American family. He said:

> I felt that an English valet would never have been so docile about being handed over to an American in payment of a poker debt. I thought he had missed

the chap's dignity. I think it was then that the idea of Jeeves came into my mind.

The name 'Jeeves' was inspired by Percy Jeeves, a Warwickshire cricketer whom Wodehouse saw playing at Cheltenham in 1913. Jeeves the manservant first appeared in print in the 1915 short story 'Extricating Young Gussie', in which he had just two lines. The following year, in 'Leave It to Jeeves', he became the mastermind we know so well. *My Man Jeeves* (1919) was the first of fifteen books that went on to make Jeeves' name a byword around the world, and for nearly sixty years he continued to get Bertie out of scrapes and unwanted engagements.

Wodehouse developed the series slowly. We do not learn of Jeeves' club, the Junior Ganymede, until *The Code of the Woosters* (1938), and we do not learn Jeeves' first name, Reginald, until *Much Obliged, Jeeves*, published on Wodehouse's 90th birthday in 1971. But one feature of Jeeves remains constant throughout the series: his omniscience. He is remarkably knowledgeable on a wide variety of subjects and uses this to extricate the young master time and time again from seemingly hopeless situations. Did Wodehouse ever know such a paragon in real life? He seems to have done so.

> *Jeeves, of course, is a gentleman's gentleman, not a butler, but if the call comes, he can buttle with the best of them. (Stiff Upper Lip, Jeeves)*

In *Bring on the Girls*, the theatrical reminiscences Wodehouse wrote with Guy Bolton, we read of an evening when Bolton dined with the Wodehouses at their house in Onslow Square. They were served by a butler named Robinson, who Wodehouse said was 'an artist's model' for the character of Jeeves. Asked to describe the home life of a type of spider, Robinson informed them that, once mating has been completed:

'... the lady has him for dinner.'
    'Nothing formal, I suppose? Just a black tie?'
    'I speak in a literal sense, sir.'
    'You mean she eats him?'
    'Precisely, sir.'

Bring on the Girls cannot be relied upon for accuracy: Wodehouse freely admitted he had changed names, dates and facts to enhance the humour. Until recently, both Robinson and Wodehouse's anecdotes concerning him were believed by some to be apocryphal. A few years ago, however, Robinson's existence was confirmed by John Millar, who had been a friend of Leonora Wodehouse in the 1920s. Millar (who had never read *Bring on the Girls*) remembered the evening and remembered Robinson, whom Wodehouse had called 'a walking *Encyclopaedia Britannica*'. When Bolton asked about the life of the African spider, Millar said:

Robinson's answer was that it was hardly a subject for mixed company and went on to explain that, after choosing and bestowing her favours on a male spider, the female spider has him for dinner. In a flash, Plum turned to Guy and said: 'Nothing formal, you understand, Guy. Just black tie.' Of course we all collapsed with laughter.

Millar remembered the butler as 'a very superior and obviously experienced man'. But, other than this recollection, no trace of Robinson has been found. Perhaps one day we shall find out more.

> *It was the soft cough of Jeeves' which always reminds me of a very old sheep clearing its throat on a distant mountain top.* (Stiff Upper Lip, Jeeves)

16

THE FINAL YEARS

WHEN THE WODEHOUSES ARRIVED in New York in 1947, they were warmly welcomed and relieved to find that the Berlin broadcasts had made little impression in the USA. They moved into an apartment at 53 East 66th Street, and Wodehouse set about resuming his career. His novel *Full Moon* had been well received, but the world had changed and the big magazines – *Saturday Evening Post* and *Collier's* – were no longer eager to publish his novels in serial form. Though his stories still sold, sixteen being published in *Playboy*, the days of large payments from magazines were over.

Wodehouse tried to revive his theatrical success but with limited results. With Guy Bolton, he rewrote *Sally* and adapted *Don't Listen, Ladies*, by Sacha Guitry, but neither did well. Later theatrical

P.G. Wodehouse with his faithful typewriter near the end of his life. (Courtesy of the late Nella Wodehouse)

work also proved disappointing and, thereafter, he concentrated on his novels, turning out roughly one a year.

In 1949 the Wodehouses moved to a penthouse at 1000 Park Avenue, which crops up as the address of Jimmy Schoonmaker in *Service with a Smile*. Three years later, while the Wodehouses were staying with Guy and Virgina Bolton at Remsenburg on the south coast of Long Island, Ethel suddenly decided to buy a house 2 miles away in Basket Neck Lane. The Wodehouses began to spend their summers there and their winters in New York.

The Wodehouses' home at Remsenburg, Long Island, New York.

In 1953 Wodehouse resumed his writing for *Punch*, turning out a fortnightly column for the next ten years. The same year also saw the publication of *Bring on the Girls* and *Performing Flea*. The former, written with Guy Bolton, is an amusing account of their years in musical comedy with superb descriptions of the larger-than-life theatrical impresarios of the period. *Performing Flea*, written with his old friend from school, Bill Townend, comprises Wodehouse's letters to Townend over the years in which Wodehouse discussed his career and constantly reviewed Townend's writing, giving him what one biographer has called 'a masterclass in literary technique'.

In 1955 the Wodehouses moved to Basket Neck Lane permanently, and on 16 December 1955, P.G. Wodehouse became an American citizen. There is speculation as to why he did this, one probable reason being that the death of Leonora meant there was less to attract him in England. He was also grateful to America, which had welcomed him after the war and where he was free from the possible prosecution he feared he could still face in England.

In 1960, as his 80th birthday approached, there was a striking tribute to Wodehouse in the press as 'an inimitable international institution and a master humorist'. It was signed by W.H. Auden, Graham Greene, John Betjeman, Nancy Mitford, Aldous Huxley, Rebecca West and Ogden Nash, amongst others. And on 15 July 1961, Evelyn Waugh broadcast a talk on the BBC, 'an act of homage and reparation' to Wodehouse, concluding with:

> Mr Wodehouse's world can never stale. He will continue to release future generations from captivity that may be more irksome than our own. He has made a world for us to live in and delight in.

In 1967 Wodehouse and Ethel established an animal shelter at nearby Westhampton. Both were animal lovers, and at Remsenburg there were always several cats and dogs in residence since neither could turn a stray away. Both knew they would never move from Remsenburg, which had appeared in *French Leave* (1956) as 'Bensonburg', and Wodehouse continued with his daily routine of physical exercises that he had performed since 1919, writing in the morning, a walk with Guy Bolton and the dogs in the afternoon, and a couple of hours' work again in the evening.

His 90th birthday produced even more fuss, but by now Wodehouse was slowing down. He was still producing a book a year but finding it harder to do so. With the exception of Guy Bolton, all his old friends were dead and there was nobody he could confide in.

In 1974 he was thrilled to learn that 'they are putting me in Madame Tussaud's which I have always looked upon as the supreme honour'. In the New Year Honours List of 1975, he was awarded a knighthood.

Towards the end of January 1975 Wodehouse began recording short introductions to the BBC TV series *Wodehouse Playhouse*, starring John Alderton and Pauline Collins. It was perhaps the result of this extra work that led him to develop pemphigus, a skin disease for which he was hospitalised for a period. On 14 February he returned for more tests, taking with him the manuscript on which he was working, subsequently published as *Sunset at Blandings*. In the evening, his doctor looked in to find him in an armchair with the manuscript beside him. At 93 years old, his heart had failed at last.

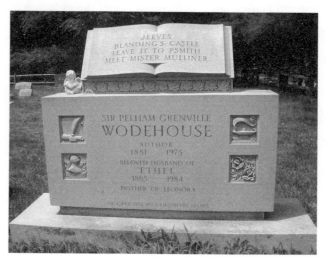

The grave of P.G. and Ethel Wodehouse at Remsenburg.

With each new book of mine I have, as I say, always that feeling that this time I have picked a lemon in the garden of literature. A good thing really, I suppose. Keeps one up on one's toes and makes one write every sentence ten times. Or in many cases twenty times. My books may not be the sort of books the cognoscenti feel justified in blowing the twelve and a half shillings on, but I do work at them. When in due course Charon ferries me across the Styx and everyone is telling everyone else what a rotten writer I was, I hope at least one voice will be heard piping up: 'But he did take trouble.' (Over Seventy)

• IMAGES •

When two men stand face to face, one of whom has recently shot the other with an airgun, and the second of whom has just discovered who did it, it is rarely that conversation flows briskly from the start.

('The Crime Wave at Blandings')

She was quite pretty in, I admit, a rather austere kind of way. She looked like a vicar's daughter who plays hockey and ticks off the villagers when they want to marry their deceased wives' sisters.

(*Laughing Gas*)

He was in the acute stage of that malady which, for want of a better name, scientists call the heeby-jeebies.

(*Spring Fever*)

Even on his good days he looked a little like something thrown off by Epstein in a particularly sombre mood, and this was not one of his good days.

(*Barmy in Wonderland*)

She unshipped a sigh that sounded like the wind going out of a rubber duck.

(*Right Ho, Jeeves*)

Honoria Glossop has a voice like a lion-tamer making some authoritative announcement to one of the troupe.

('Without the Option')

'Well,' she said, choking on the word like a Pekinese on a chump chop too large for its frail strength.

(*Jeeves and the Feudal Spirit*)

There was a crackling sound, like a forest fire, as Mr Steptoe champed his toast. This gorilla-jawed man could get a certain amount of noise response even out of mashed potatoes, but it was when eating toast that you caught him at his best.

(*Quick Service*)

A wooden expression had crept into his features, and his eyes had taken on the look of cautious reserve which you see in those of parrots, when offered half a banana by a stranger of whose bona fides they are not convinced.

(*Joy in the Morning*)

It would take more than long-stemmed roses to change my view that you're a despicable cowardy custard and a disgrace to a proud family. Your ancestors fought in the Crusades and were often mentioned in despatches, and you cringe like a salted snail at the thought of appearing as Santa Claus before an audience of charming children who wouldn't hurt a fly. It's enough to make an aunt turn her face to the wall and give up the struggle.

('*Jeeves and the Greasy Bird*')

17

A WODEHOUSE TIMELINE

1881	**15 October:** *Pelham 'Plum' Grenville Wodehouse is born to Eleanor Deane Wodehouse at 1 Ash Vale Place (now 59 Epsom Road), Guildford, the third of four brothers.*
	Wodehouse is taken out to Hong Kong, where his father, Henry Ernest Wodehouse, is a magistrate.
1883–1894	*The three brothers — Peveril, Armine and Pelham — return to England and are placed in the care of a governess in Bath, followed by a dame school in Croydon, then Elizabeth College in Guernsey. Plum is then sent to Malvern House, Dover.*
1894	*Wodehouse enters Dulwich College; his brother Armine had entered two years before.*

1896	*Wodehouse's parents return to the UK and, after renting a house in Dulwich for a short period, take a lease on the Old House, Stableford, Shropshire. He joins them there for school holidays.*
1900	*Wodehouse plays for the First XV and First XI, and becomes an editor of the school magazine, The Alleynian. He receives 10s 6d from the Public School Magazine for 'Some Aspects of Game-Captaincy'.*
	September: *Wodehouse joins the Hong Kong and Shanghai Bank in Lombard Street, London, and takes lodgings in Markham Square, Chelsea.*
	November: *His first humorous article, 'Men Who Have Missed Their Own Weddings', appears in Tit-Bits.*
1902	*Wodehouse's parents leave Shropshire and move to Cheltenham. About this time, he takes lodgings at 23 Walpole Street, Chelsea.*
	September: *Wodehouse leaves the bank and becomes a freelance writer. His first article appears in Punch, and his first book, The Pothunters, is published. (He will publish six more school novels until his last, Mike, in 1909.)*

1903	*Wodehouse secures the position of assistant on the By The Way column of The Globe evening newspaper. He plays for the Authors' cricket team with Conan Doyle.*
	Late in the year Herbert Westbrook arrives with a letter of introduction and invites Wodehouse to stay at Emsworth House School.
1904	*Wodehouse spends his annual leave on a short visit to New York. Upon his return, he rents 'Threepwood' in Emsworth.*
	***August:** Wodehouse becomes editor of the By The Way column at £5 a week.*
	***December:** He writes the lyric for 'Put Me In My Little Cell' for the show Sergeant Brue, the first of hundreds of lyrics he would write over the next thirty years.*
1905	***July:** His first story in The Strand magazine, 'The Wire-Pullers', appears.*
1906	***March:** Seymour Hicks, actor-manager, engages Wodehouse to write topical lyrics. He meets Jerome Kern for the first time.*
	Love Among the Chickens is published.
1907	***December:** The Gaiety Theatre engages Wodehouse as lyricist.*
1909	***May:** Wodehouse makes his second visit to New York; he sells two magazine stories for $500 and resigns from The Globe.*

	September: *Mike, which introduces Rupert Psmith, is published in the UK.*
1910	*Wodehouse returns to England in February, sails again to New York in March and back once more to England in May. There will be many further trips to the US.*
1911	**24 August:** *A Gentleman of Leisure, Wodehouse's first play, opens in New York.*
1913	*His play Brother Alfred flops in London.*
1914	**August:** *Wodehouse arrives in New York; he meets widow Ethel Wayman.*
	30 September: *Wodehouse marries Ethel (b. 23 May 1885) at The Little Church Around the Corner, New York. They subsequently rent a house at Bellport, Long Island.*
1915	*Wodehouse becomes drama critic for Vanity Fair (US) magazine.*
	1 March: *The film of A Gentleman of Leisure made in the USA.*
1915	**26 June:** *Something New begins in the Saturday Evening Post.*
1915	**18 September:** *Jeeves makes his first appearance in 'Extricating Young Gussie'.*
1916	**25 September:** *Miss Springtime, by Bolton, Wodehouse & Kern, opens in New York.*

1917	The trio continue their Broadway success with *Have a Heart, Oh, Boy!, Leave It to Jane, The Riviera Girl* and *Miss 1917*.
1918	*Oh, Lady! Lady!!, See You Later, The Girl Behind the Gun, The Canary* and *Oh, My Dear!* all do well in New York.
	The Wodehouses move to Great Neck, Long Island; Wodehouse plays golf at the Sound View course.
1919	Wodehouse returns to London but travels to New York frequently over the next ten years.
1922	**19 September:** *The Cabaret Girl*, written with George Grossmith Jr, opens in London.
1923	Wodehouse travels to East Hampton, Long Island, for six months, then returns to the UK.
	5 September: *The Beauty Prize* opens in London.
1924	The Wodehouses visit Paris and Harrogate, then take a house in Gilbert Street, London.
	December: Wodehouse's first visit to Hunstanton Hall, Norfolk, for Christmas.
1926	Wodehouse undertakes more visits to Hunstanton Hall. These continue until 1933.
	December: The Wodehouses move to 17 Norfolk Street (now Dunraven Street).

1929	**27 May:** *Father, Henry Ernest Wodehouse, dies at Bexhill-on-Sea.*
	30 September: *Candle-Light opens in New York.*
	November: *Wodehouse makes a short visit to Hollywood and agrees a contract for one year with MGM.*
1930	**8 May:** *Wodehouse and Leonora arrive in Hollywood.*
1931	**7 June:** *Interview with Wodehouse appears in the Los Angeles Times.*
	September: *Wodehouse returns to London and rents 19 Grosvenor Mews.*
1932	*The Wodehouses rent a house near Cannes for a year.*
	12 December: *Leonora Wodehouse marries Peter Cazalet.*
1934	**31 March:** *Sheran Cazalet is born.*
	June: *The Wodehouses move to Le Touquet.*
	August: *Wodehouse rents Low Wood, Le Touquet, which he will buy a year later.*
1936	**26 April:** *Edward Cazalet is born.*
	10 October: *Wodehouse returns to Hollywood on contract to MGM.*
1937	**May:** *He adapts A Damsel in Distress for the screen.*
	November: *Wodehouse returns to Low Wood.*

1939	**21 June:** *Wodehouse is made Honorary Doctor of Literature by Oxford University.*
	July: *Wodehouse visits Dulwich for the last time to watch a cricket match.*
	September: *The Second World War begins; during the 'phoney war' British residents in northern France are advised to stay where they are.*
1940	**May:** *As German armoured divisions sweep through northern France, the Wodehouses make two attempts to escape. The Germans occupy Le Touquet.*
	July: *Wodehouse is taken with other British males to the prison at Loos, then to Liège, then to Huy and finally to a former lunatic asylum at Tost in Upper Silesia.*
1941	**17 February:** *Mother, Eleanor Deane Wodehouse, dies in Maidenhead.*
	21 June: *Wodehouse is released and taken to the Adlon Hotel, Berlin, where he meets two pre-war acquaintances, one of whom now works for the German Foreign Office. It is suggested Wodehouse gives some talks on radio on his experiences to neutral America. He goes on to make five recordings.*

	15 July: *William O'Connor broadcasts an attack on Wodehouse on the BBC, accusing him of being a traitor. This will cast a shadow over Wodehouse for the rest of his life.*
1943	***7 September:*** *The Wodehouses are allowed to leave for Paris.*
1944	***16 May:*** *Leonora dies. The Wodehouses do not hear of it until September.*
	9 September: *Major Cussen of MI5 begins interrogation of Wodehouse.*
	23 November: *Cussen's report clears Wodehouse sufficiently for the Director of Public Prosecutions to say prosecution would not be justified.*
1945	*The Second World War ends; Wodehouse and his wife stay on in Paris.*
1947	***26 April:*** *The Wodehouses arrive in New York.*
1948	***2 September:*** *Don't Listen, Ladies! opens at St James's Theatre, London.*
1952	***June:*** *While visiting Guy and Virginia Bolton at Remsenburg, Long Island, Ethel Wodehouse buys a house at Basket Neck Lane, 2 miles away. For the next three years, the Wodehouses spend the summers there and winters at Park Avenue.*
1953	***July:*** *Wodehouse renews his association with Punch in a series of articles.*

1955	**April:** *The Wodehouses move permanently to Remsenburg.*
	16 December: *Wodehouse becomes an American citizen.*
1961	*Wodehouse is lauded by fellow writers, including Evelyn Waugh, on the occasion of his 80th birthday.*
1965	**May:** *The World of Wooster TV series begins, with Ian Carmichael and Dennis Price.*
1967	**February:** *Blandings Castle TV series with Ralph Richardson.*
1967	*P.G. Wodehouse Animal Shelter opens at Remsenburg. (It is now a Bide-a-Wee shelter.)*
1971	**15 October:** *More tributes as Wodehouse turns 90.*
1974	*Aunts Aren't Gentlemen, Wodehouse's last complete novel, is published.*
1975	**January:** *Wodehouse receives a knighthood.*
	14 February: *Sir Pelham Grenville Wodehouse dies in hospital with a manuscript at his bedside.*
1977	*Sunset at Blandings, the unfinished novel Wodehouse was working on when he died, is published, annotated by Richard Usborne.*
1984	**6 October:** *Ethel Wodehouse dies.*

18

THE WODEHOUSE INFLUENCE

THE ENDURING APPEAL OF P.G. Wodehouse's writing is such that he continues to be quoted in the press almost daily. His influence has reached into many areas, including the law: in 2006 a law journal reported increasing use of the term 'the Bertie Wooster escape clause'. This summarises the principle of English law that unearned income is ignored in determining liability for child support.

Wodehouse's writing has been translated into more than thirty languages, including French, Swedish, Italian, Hungarian, Japanese, and Arabic. Fans worldwide have commemorated him in a variety of ways – some of them highly unusual.

• PLAQUES •

A blue plaque, unveiled by the Queen Mother, identifies Wodehouse's house at 17 Dunraven Street, London, while an unofficial plaque marks his earlier stay at Walton Street, South Kensington. Wodehouse's birthplace in Epsom Road, Guildford, has a plaque, as does 'Threepwood', his house in Record Road, Emsworth.

The Wodehouse Society (USA) has placed a plaque in The Little Church Around the Corner, New York, commemorating his marriage there in 1914, and in 2012 erected a marker near his grave at Remsenburg.

In France, on the wall of the Villa Lambins-Lalanne, Les Lambins, Avenue de Trepied, Le Touquet, is a black marble plaque to Wodehouse. The house – which, it is said, is the only one in Le Touquet that has remained in English hands since before the war – stands next door to the Wodehouses' villa.

A plaque at Zutphen, the Netherlands, erected by the Dutch P.G. Wodehouse Society, commemorates Sir Philip Sidney and his fellow author and compatriot P.G. Wodehouse.

The Belgian Drones Club installed a plaque at the Citadel at Huy that recalls Wodehouse's internment

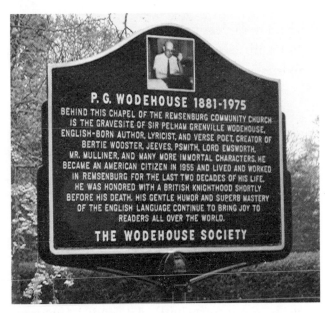

Plaque in front of the church in Remsenburg, erected by The Wodehouse Society (USA).

there in 1940. They have also presented a plaque which is now in the dining room of the Hong Kong and Shanghai Bank's London headquarters.

• STREET NAMES •

One section of Newport Pagnell, Buckinghamshire, has streets named after famous writers, including a Wodehouse Walk. Guildford, Surrey, has named a small alley Wodehouse Place; it is just a few yards from his birthplace at 59 Epsom Road. There is also a Wodehouse Road in Hunstanton, Norfolk.

• ADOPTION OF CHARACTER NAMES •

Keen Wodehouseans have applied or adapted his character names to their own fields of interest. For example, members of Wodehouse societies and online discussion groups often assume a 'nom de Plum' to communicate with each other.

In December 1988, *Donald Duck Adventures* featured Sir Bertrand Wister, Earl of Enthouse. A later edition, October 1997, had Donald Duck graduating from the 'Wodehouse Butler Academy' and becoming butler to the Chief Examiner 'Lord Glossop'.

The author Arthur Ransome was so impressed by the character of Lottie Blossom (*The Luck of the Bodkins*) that he named his new sailing boat after her. Wodehouse was delighted by the compliment.

Horse racing has seen numerous Wodehousean names. The *Daily Telegraph* of 3 July 1989 tipped 'Bertie Wooster' for the 3.45 at Pontefract. In July 1992 he won the Palan Handicap as a 9 year old: 'Bertie Wooster, who won this same sprint four years ago, showed there is still fire in the belly when producing a great final furlong . . . and winning by a length and a half.' His owner, Miss Rawding, clearly had the right spirit in her — she also owned 'P. Smith' and 'Aunt Agatha'!

In other races, 'Gussie Fink-Nottle' (owner Mrs S. Sturman) came second in the Everest Maiden Stakes at Edinburgh in 1992. And in 1996 a newspaper noted the current generation of 'Wodehorses' were not doing too well: 'Plum First', 'Winsome Wooster' and 'Pelham' had only achieved four placings in eighteen races: one first, two seconds and one third. However, on 14 November 2002, 'Madeline Bassett' won at Lingfield Park at 7–1.

Wodehouse has been commemorated in the world of horticulture as well. Jim Durrant of McBean's Orchids (Lewes, Sussex) has bred orchids to produce new crosses named after Wodehouse characters. These include *Christmas Cheer* 'Aunt Dahlia', *Loch Leven* 'Bertie Wooster', and *Loch Leven* 'Jeeves'. There is also an orchid variety called Blandings, and one named after Wodehouse himself.

In October 1991, on the 110th anniversary of Wodehouse's birth, the Dutch Wodehouse Society formally named seven new dahlias. The

P.G. Wodehouse Memorial Collection of dahlias, developed by Cor Geerlings, were named P.G. Wodehouse, Aunt Dahlia, Milady's Boudoir, Jeeves, Bertie Wooster, Uncle Fred and Sir Philip Sidney. And a new red rose with a yellow centre, *Rosa Sir Pelham Grenville Wodehouse*, was registered in The Netherlands in 1996.

When I 'edited' the Hon. Galahad Threepwood's *Reminiscences*, the Public Lending Rights organisation asked for the address of the co-author. It needed two letters to convince them that the Hon. Galahad was a fictional creation.

But perhaps the most amusing use of a Wodehouse character was by a Washington DC businessman named Peter Sinclair. In the late 1990s, tired of dealing with cold calls and visiting salesmen, Mr Sinclair began telling them that their query was being dealt with by J. Fillken Wilberfloss (a character in *Psmith Journalist*). Mr Wilberfloss was unfortunately 'on holiday at present', 'visiting branches out of town', or 'in conference'. Eventually Mr Wilberfloss developed a life of his own. His name began to appear on mailing lists; invitations to trade functions started to arrive. When last heard of, Mr Wilberfloss was being asked to forward details of his career for inclusion in reference books.

• WINING AND DINING •

In the village of Copythorne, just north of Southampton, Hampshire, is a pub named 'Empress of Blandings'. A superb painting of the Empress adorns the outside, while inside are a splendid collection of Wodehouse dust covers, shelves of his books, and porcine memorabilia wherever one looks.

Mulliner's Wijnlokaal, a wine bar in Amsterdam, sells 'Mister Mulliner's Port' and is the meeting place of the Dutch Wodehouse Society.

Drones, a restaurant at 1 Pont Street, London (founded 1972), asked Wodehouse's permission to use the name, which he was happy to give. There is also The Drones Club, a live music club in north London and The Drones Comedy Club, Chapter Arts Centre, Cardiff.

In 1988 John Gilbert of the Hop Back Brewery, Salisbury, was asked to provide a beer for the Salisbury Beer Festival. He created a special brew and named it after the book he was reading at the time – *Summer Lightning*.

• SOCIETY VENTURES •

In both the Philadelphia Zoo and Boston's Franklin Park Zoo, there is a glass tank providing domicile to various families of newts. On each tank is a plaque recording the sponsorship of the tanks by, respectively, Chapter One (Philadelphia) and the NEWTS (Boston), chapters of The Wodehouse Society (US) – a salute to newt-loving Gussie Fink-Nottle.

The US Society also has a cricket club; they sport a badge of crossed cricket bats surmounted by a pig with the motto *Risus, Vestimenta, Conviva* (Laughter, Clothing, Conviviality).

The Gold Bats of the UK Society play an annual match against the masters of Dulwich College (The Dusters). They also play The Gentlemen of the Sherlock Holmes Society of London in a match conducted under the 1895 rules of cricket.

• COMMERCIAL VENTURES •

The name of Jeeves has become ubiquitous, even being appropriated for a search engine (Ask Jeeves). Branches of the dry-cleaning firm Jeeves of Belgravia are a common sight around London, while Jeeves Tours operate in Christchurch, New

Zealand. Jeeves and Jericho of Witney sell quality teas of every description, and the S. Constantos Distillery in Crete has produced 'Jeeves Gin', a bottle of which I bought in 1987. *The Jeeves Cocktail Book* was published by Ebury Press in 1980. Today, Levenger (USA) sell the Jeeves, a small filing cabinet doubling as a footrest, with a padded top that can be used as a lap desk.

A firm called 'Blandings' specialises in renting beautiful houses in Britain for weekend parties and holiday stays. Their larger properties, suitable for eighteen to twenty people, cost £5,000 for a Friday to Monday stay.

Unable to find a china figure of the Infant Samuel to smash in moments of stress, Rosalie Frudakis of Pennsylvania commissioned her niece, sculptor Jennifer Frudakis, to make some. I am the proud owner of model No. 1.

• THE GUTENBERG BIBLE IN THE BLANDINGS CASTLE LIBRARY •

Robert Birley, headmaster of Eton (1949–63), had a great admiration for Wodehouse. In his 1970 booklet on the 100 most interesting books in the Eton library, he included its rare Gutenberg Bible, one of forty-eight in the world. In the middle of the description, he inserted: 'To the recorded copies of the Gutenberg Bible should be added one in the library of Blandings Castle in Shropshire.' In a letter to Wodehouse, he said he hoped he would be approached by some German professor 'to whom I shall suggest he catches the 11.18 or 2.30 train from Paddington Station to Market Blandings'.

19

BOOKS BY P.G. WODEHOUSE

US titles in brackets; * published posthumously

· SCHOOL STORIES ·

1902	*The Pothunters*
1903	*A Prefect's Uncle*
	Tales of St Austin's
1904	*The Gold Bat*
1905	*The Head of Kay's*
1907	*The White Feather*
1919	*Mike* [first Psmith story]
1997*	*Tales of Wrykyn and Elsewhere*

Wodehouse's first published book.

• CHILDREN'S / PARODY / MISCELLANEOUS •

1904   *William Tell Told Again*
1908   *The Globe By The Way Book*
1909   *The Swoop!*

• PSMITH •

1909   *Mike* [school story]
1910   *Psmith in the City*
1915   *Psmith Journalist*
1923   *Leave It to Psmith*

• UKRIDGE •

1906   *Love Among the Chickens* (rev. 1921)
1924   *Ukridge (He Rather Enjoyed It)*

• BLANDINGS CASTLE •

1915   *Something Fresh (Something New)*
1923   *Leave It to Psmith*
1929   *Summer Lightning (Fish Preferred)*
1933   *Heavy Weather*
1939   *Uncle Fred in the Springtime*
1947   *Full Moon*

• JEEVES AND WOOSTER •

Wodehouse's last completed book, published in 1974.

1953	*Ring for Jeeves* (*The Return of Jeeves*)
1954	*Jeeves and the Feudal Spirit* (*Bertie Wooster Sees It Through*
1960	*Jeeves in the Offing* (*How Right You Are, Jeeves*)
1963	*Stiff Upper Lip, Jeeves*
1971	*Much Obliged, Jeeves* (*Jeeves and the Tie That Binds*)
1974	*Aunts Aren't Gentlemen* (*The Catnappers*)

GOLF STORIES

| 1922 | *The Clicking of Cuthbert* (*Golf Without Tears*) |
| 1926 | *The Heart of a Goof* (*Divots*) |

MR MULLINER

1927	*Meet Mr Mulliner*
1929	*Mr Mulliner Speaking*
1933	*Mulliner Nights*

MONTY BODKIN

1933	*Heavy Weather* [Blandings novel]
1935	*The Luck of the Bodkins*
1972	*Pearls, Girls and Monty Bodkin* (*The Plot That Thickened*)

• LIGHT NOVELS •

1907   *Not George Washington*

1910   *A Gentleman of Leisure (The Intrusion of Jimmy)*

1912   *The Prince and Betty*

1913   *The Little Nugget*

1916   *Uneasy Money*

1917   *Piccadilly Jim*

1919   *The Coming of Bill (Their Mutual Child)*
       A Damsel in Distress

1921   *Jill the Reckless (The Little Warrior)*
       Indiscretions of Archie

1922   *The Girl on the Boat (Three Men and a Maid)*
       The Adventures of Sally (Mostly Sally)

1924   *Bill the Conqueror*

1925   *Sam the Sudden (Sam in the Suburbs)*

1927   *The Small Bachelor*

1928   *Money for Nothing*

1931   *Big Money*
       If I Were You

1932   *Doctor Sally*
       Hot Water

1936   *Laughing Gas*

1937   *Summer Moonshine*

1940   *Quick Service*

1942   *Money in the Bank*

1948	*Spring Fever*
	Uncle Dynamite
1951	*The Old Reliable*
1952	*Barmy in Wonderland (Angel Cake)*
1956	*French Leave*
1957	*Something Fishy (The Butler Did It)*
1958	*Cocktail Time*
1961	*Ice in the Bedroom (The Ice in the Bedroom)*
1964	*Frozen Assets (Biffen's Millions)*
1967	*Company for Henry (The Purloined Paperweight)*
1968	*Do Butlers Burgle Banks?*
1970	*The Girl in Blue*
1973	*Bachelors Anonymous*

• SHORT STORY COLLECTIONS •

1914	*The Man Upstairs*
1917	*The Man with Two Left Feet* [Includes first Bertie & Jeeves story]
1935	*Blandings Castle* [Blandings & Mr Mulliner stories]
1936	*Young Men in Spats* [Drones Club & Mr Mulliner stories]
1937	*Lord Emsworth and Others* (*The Crime Wave at Blandings*) [Blandings, Mr Mulliner & Ukridge stories]

1940 *Eggs, Beans and Crumpets* [Drones, Mr Mulliner & Ukridge stories]

1950 *Nothing Serious* [Drones, Blandings, golf & Ukridge stories]

1959 *A Few Quick Ones* [Mr Mulliner, Drones & golf stories]

1966 *Plum Pie* [Jeeves, golf, Blandings, Ukridge & Drones stories]

1991* *A Man of Means*

• AUTOBIOGRAPHICAL WORKS •

1953 *Performing Flea (Author! Author!)*

1954 *Bring on the Girls*

• COLLECTED MAGAZINE ARTICLES •

1932 *Louder and Funnier*

1957 *Over Seventy (America, I Like You)*

• POETRY •

1988* *The Parrot and Other Poems*

2014* *What Goes Around Comes Around*

20

WODEHOUSE ON THE STAGE

· MUSICALS ·

The musicals listed below are those for which Wodehouse wrote lyrics and/or the book.

1904   *Sergeant Brue* (London)
1906   *The Beauty of Bath* (London)
1907   *The Gay Gordons* (London)
          The Bandit's Daughter (London)
1914   *Nuts and Wine* (London)
1916   *Pom Pom* (New York)
          Miss Springtime (New York)
1917   *Have a Heart* (New York)
          Oh, Boy! (New York)
          Leave It to Jane (New York)

	Kitty Darlin' (New York)
	The Riviera Girl (New York)
	Miss 1917 (New York)
1918	*Oh, Lady! Lady!!* (New York)
	See You Later (New York)
	The Girl Behind the Gun (New York)
	The Canary (New York)
	Oh, My Dear! (New York)
1919	*The Rose of China* (New York)
1920	*Sally* (New York)
1921	*The Golden Moth* (London)
1922	*The Cabaret Girl* (London)
1923	*The Beauty Prize* (London)
1924	*Sitting Pretty* (New York)
1926	*Hearts and Diamonds* (London)
	Oh, Kay! (New York)
1927	*The Nightingale* (New York)
	Show Boat (New York)
1928	*Rosalie* (New York)
	The Three Musketeers (New York)
1934	*Anything Goes* (New York)

• WODEHOUSE PLAYS •

In addition to the musical comedies for which he
wrote lyrics and, often, the libretto, Wodehouse

wrote and adapted many plays. Several were never staged; the following list shows only those that were produced.

1911 *A Gentleman of Leisure* (New York)

1913 *Brother Alfred* (London)

1914 *Brother Fans* (New York)

1920 *Piccadilly Jim* (Washington, DC)

1926 *The Play's the Thing* (New York; also London in 1928)

1927 *Her Cardboard Lover* (New York & London)
      Good Morning, Bill (London)

1928 *A Damsel in Distress* (London)

1929 *Baa, Baa, Black Sheep* (London)
      Candle-Light (New York)

1930 *Leave It to Psmith* (London)

1934 *Who's Who* (London)

1935 *The Inside Stand* (London)

1948 *Don't Listen, Ladies!* (London & New York)

1950 *Don't Lose Your Head* (UK provincial theatres)
      Nothing Serious (on tour US)

1954 *Joy in the Morning* (Ashburton, South Devon)

1957 *Come On, Jeeves* (Cambridge, UK)

1978 *Arthur* (New York; posthumous)

21

WODEHOUSE FILMS
AND TELEVISION PLAYS

• SILENT FILMS •

1915	*A Gentleman of Leisure* (US)
1918	*Uneasy Money* (US)
1919	*Oh, Boy!* (US)
	A Damsel in Distress (US)
	The Prince and Betty (US)
	Piccadilly Jim (US)
1920	*Their Mutual Child* (US)
	Oh, Lady, Lady (US)
1923	*A Gentleman of Leisure* (US)
1924	*The Clicking of Cuthbert* (UK, six golf stories)
1925	*Sally* (US)
1927	*The Small Bachelor* (US)
1928	*The Cardboard Lover* (US)
	Oh, Kay! (US)

• FILMS WITH SOUND •

1929	*Sally* (US, colour)
	Her Cardboard Lover (UK, 5 minutes)
1930	*Those Three French Girls* (US)
1932	*Brother Alfred* (UK)
1933	*Leave it to Me* (UK)
	By Candlelight (US)
	Summer Lightning (UK)
1936	*Anything Goes* (US)
	Piccadilly Jim (US)
	Thank You, Jeeves! (US)
1937	*Step Lively, Jeeves!* (US)
	A Damsel in Distress (US)
1942	*Her Cardboard Lover* (US)
1956	*Anything Goes* (US)
1961	*The Girl on the Boat* (UK)
2006	*Piccadilly Jim* (UK)

• TELEVISION ADAPTATIONS •

1949	*By Candlelight* (UK)
1953	*Uncle Fred Flits By* (US, also 1955)
1956	*Lord Emsworth and the Little Friend* (UK)
1965–67	*The World of Wooster* (series, UK, twenty episodes)

Stephen Fry and Hugh Laurie as Jeeves and Bertie Wooster in the 1990s BBC TV series *Jeeves & Wooster*.

22

WODEHOUSE SOCIETIES WORLDWIDE

THE P.G. WODEHOUSE SOCIETY (UK)

http://www.pgwodehousesociety.org.uk/

Founded in 1997 and comprising over 1,000 members, this society has a quarterly journal, *Wooster Sauce*; holds three meetings a year in London as well as a biennial formal dinner; conducts occasional special events such as A Week With Wodehouse; and sponsors a campaign to Back the Berkshire, in honour of the Empress of Blandings.

THE WODEHOUSE SOCIETY

http://www.wodehouse.org/

The North American society, formed in 1980, currently has over 650 members, many of whom have formed regional chapters. TWS publishes a quarterly journal, *Plum Lines*, and holds biennial conventions (odd-numbered years) in a different city each time. Their website includes information on joining PGWnet, a Wodehouse discussion forum.

THE P.G. WODEHOUSE SOCIETY (NETHERLANDS)

http://www.wodehouse-society.nl/

Though the Dutch group officially formed in 1981, one of the founders possesses a letter from Wodehouse, dated 1973, in which he gave his formal permission for them to create a society in his honour. The group meets regularly at Mulliner's Wijnlokaal in Amsterdam and publishes a journal, *Nothing Serious*.

THE RUSSIAN WODEHOUSE SOCIETY

http://wodehouse.ru/index.htm

The Russian society is run by dedicated Wodehouseans who have accumulated an array of articles, photos, and resources on their website, which can be viewed in Russian or English.

THE SWEDISH WODEHOUSE SOCIETY

http://www.wodehouse.se/

With over 200 members, the Swedish society issues

a journal entitled *Blandings Blandning* (Blandings Mixture) and a yearbook called *Jeeves*.

Les Amis de Plum

http://wodehouse-fr.tumblr.com/asso
This French group aims to bring together francophone admirers of Wodehouse. "Our goal is to share and perpetuate the joy and the giggles which are so common while reading his narratives."

Other groups of Wodehouse fans can be found in Belgium, Finland, Italy, India and Australia. Contact information can be found on the US Society's website.

23

RECOMMENDED WODEHOUSE WEBSITES

(See also Wodehouse Societies Worldwide)

MADAME EULALIE'S RARE PLUMS
www.madameulalie.org/
This excellent site is dedicated to Wodehouse's early writings (pre-1923). It includes stories and articles that have not been republished in books – a real treasure trove for Wodehouse fans. Madame Eulalie also hosts 'A Celebration of P. G. Wodehouse', created by the late Terry Mordue, which includes general information on Wodehouse, bibliographies, and annotations of many of his stories; and 'Biblia Wodehousiana', created by Fr Rob Bovendeaard to track and explain Wodehouse's biblical quotations and allusions.

NEIL MIDKIFF'S P. G. WODEHOUSE PAGES
home.earthlink.net/~nmidkiff/pgw/
For comprehensive lists of Wodehouse's short stories and novels, you can't do better than this website. There is also a 'starter' Wodehouse quiz.

P.G. WODEHOUSE – 'THE OFFICIAL SITE'
http://www.wodehouse.co.uk/
This website is maintained by Arrow Books, a division of Random House that publishes Wodehouse titles in paperback. It includes information about Wodehouse, a 'cocktail recommender', and a quote generator.

PLUMTOPIA: THE WORLD OF P.G. WODEHOUSE
honoriaplum.wordpress.com/
'Honoria Glossop' is a writer from New Zealand, now based in England, whose interesting blog covers various aspects of the Wodehouse canon.

P. G. WODEHOUSE PÅ SVENSKA
http://www.wodehousebibliografier.n.nu/
Two Swedes, Tomas Prenkert and Bengt Malmberg, created this website covering all aspects of Wodehouse in Swedish – books, anthologies, articles, films and more. See also their companion

website, *Wodehouseforskning / Sverige* at http://
wodehouseforskning.weebly.com/. Both sites
include English translations.

A WODEHOUSE PAGE

http://www.borgos.nndata.no/wodehouse.htm
Created by Johna I. Borgos, a Norwegian, this page
includes some interesting information on translations into Norwegian and Swedish.

P.G. WODEHOUSE PAGE

http://www.revbiro.hu/pgw.htm
Demonstrating Wodehouse's universal appeal, this
page is the work of Révbíró Tamás, a Hungarian
whose photographs include book covers of titles
translated into Hungarian.

A SELECTED WODEHOUSE BIBLIOGRAPHY

Connolly, Joseph, *P.G. Wodehouse* (Thames & Hudson, 1979)

Davis, Lee, *Bolton and Wodehouse and Kern* (James H. Heineman Inc., 1993)

Day, Barry, *The Complete Lyrics of P.G. Wodehouse* (Scarecrow, Oxford Publicity Partnership, 2004)

Donaldson, Frances, *P.G. Wodehouse: A Biography* (Weidenfeld and Nicholson, 1974)

Edwards, O.D., *P.G. Wodehouse* (Martin Brian & O'Keefe, 1977)

French, R.B.D., *P.G. Wodehouse* (Oliver & Boyd, 1966)

Green, Benny, *P.G. Wodehouse: A Literary Biography* (Pavilion Books, 1981)

Hedgcock, Murray (ed.), *Wodehouse at the Wicket* (Hutchinson, 1997; Arrow, 2011)

Jaggard, G., *Blandings the Blest* (Macdonald & Co., 1968)

——, *Wooster's World* (Macdonald & Co., 1967)

McCrum, Robert, *Wodehouse: A Life* (Viking, 2004)

McIlvaine, E., *P.G. Wodehouse, A Comprehensive Bibliography and Checklist* (James H. Heineman, Inc., 1990)

Murphy, N.T.P., *In Search of Blandings* (Secker & Warburg, 1986)

——, *A Wodehouse Handbook*, rev. ed. (Sybertooth, 2013)

Ratcliffe, Sophie (ed.), *P.G. Wodehouse: A Life in Letters* (Hutchinson, 2011)

Ring, Tony, *Second Row, Grand Circle: A Reference Guide to the Contribution of P G Wodehouse to the Legitimate Theatre* (Harebrain Publishing, 2012)

Sproat, Iain, *Wodehouse at War* (Milner and Company, 1981)

Taves, Brian, *P.G. Wodehouse and Hollywood* (McFarland & Co., 2006)

Usborne, R., *Wodehouse at Work* (Herbert Jenkins, 1961)

——, *Wodehouse at Work to the End* (Barrie & Jenkins, 1976)

Wind, H.W., *The World of P.G. Wodehouse* (Hutchinson, 1981)

Also available in this series:

"If anyone writes about
my life in the future,
I'd rather they got the
facts right." *Agatha Christie*

THE
Agatha Christie
MISCELLANY

CATHY COOK

978 0 7524 7960 6